DEADLY!

DEADLY!

DOUG ELLIS

SPORTS PROJECTS

•

First published in Great Britain in 1998 by
SPORTS PROJECTS LTD
188 Lightwoods Hill, Smethwick, Warley, West Midlands B67 5EH
www.sportsprojects.com

•

ISBN 0 946866 47 3

•

•

A catalogue record for this book is available from the British Library

•

Printed in Great Britain

Contents

Dedication

I was three years old when my father died, leaving my mother as a young widow in the aftermath of World War I, and with very sparse means of support. Like other ladies of that era, when a generation of husbands and sons had been decimated by war, my mum simply had to cope, without the help of the welfare state as it exists today.

As a widow with two young children to support, she had to find ways of earning a living. She took in a lodger to bring in a few shillings a week. She also took in washing and I have hazy memories of helping her by turning the handle on the old-fashioned mangle.

I was heartbroken when she died and will always regret realising too late that all she really wanted in return for the start she gave me in life, against all the odds of those difficult days, was more of my time.

The story of my life is dedicated to her memory.

DOUG ELLIS, Spring 1998

Foreword

by Paul McGrath

Before I joined Aston Villa from Manchester United I had heard that the club's chairman, Doug Ellis, was known throughout football as 'Deadly', but that was about all I knew of him.

Looking back now, eight years and two clubs later, I can only say that I had by far the closest relationship with him than any other football director I have ever known.

If the term 'Deadly' was intended as in any way a critical one, then it certainly did not fit the person with whom I had dealings.

Doug Ellis was always brilliant to me, a father figure I guess, someone whose office door was always open and who had a sympathetic ear whenever I felt I had a problem to discuss.

To be honest, I did have a few low moments in my life at that time and I did go to see him whenever I felt I needed a chat. If he could, he would always help.

This was how I found it from my very first dealings with Aston Villa FC. When I left Old Trafford I had no agent to advise me, so I was a little apprehensive about how I would be treated when I talked to the manager Graham Taylor and Mr Ellis.

I need not have worried at all. I was immediately impressed with how they worked together for the club and I certainly need not have worried about how my contract talks would progress.

The fact was I came out with a better deal than I expected and that, remember, was without an agent's help. I was more than satisfied.

Once at Villa Park Doug Ellis was always very, very straight with me and I was deeply sorry when the time came for me to leave.

Recently I was discussing things with my wife Caroline and we both agreed that if there were one club I would be happy to go back to it would be Aston Villa. The time I spent at Villa Park were the best and happiest years of my entire career.

It gives me great pleasure to be able to make my feelings known in the introduction to Doug Ellis's life story, which I am sure will attract enormous interest.

PAUL McGRATH

Prologue

by Dennis Shaw

On the evening of Thursday November 21st, 1968, a militant gathering of nearly a thousand disgruntled Aston Villa supporters assembled at the Digbeth Civic Hall, near the centre of Birmingham.

Their objective was to demonstrate to the club's board of directors that the patience of those fans who cared most deeply had finally snapped.

This was no rabble-rousing mob comprised of troublemakers bent on causing mischief. Indeed, the rather unlikely rebel leader was a mild-mannered, courteous, professional man named Brian Evans, whose sincere aim was to see that the club he supported was steered away from impending financial disaster.

For a considerable time unrest among the public had been gaining strength. The Aston Villa Shareholders' Association had put up a 'Shadow Board', similar to an opposition political party. Other groups were ready to bid for power and the local *Evening Mail* had published a blunt open letter to the directors urging them to resign. All this was taking place as the club became insolvent, with liabilities outstripping assets and the bank manager threatening to call in the overdraft. The public meeting was simply a catalyst for all the various forces working against the directors, but what a perfectly timed one it proved to be.

Before the meeting could get down to its protesting a letter was delivered from the Aston Villa President, Sir Theodore Pritchett, saying in effect that directors were now prepared to sell shares and move over.

Suddenly, a meeting which when called had seemed to be merely part of a war of attrition, had become as significant in the club's history as the famous pioneering lamplight discussions among Aston Villa's founders in 1874. Those meetings led to the 'old' Aston Villa being formed. The Digbeth gathering led to the club walking away from the past, magnificent though it had been, and into a new world that was changing at a bewildering rate. Events moved in torrents once the dam had been breached, but not without controversy and dispute flooding in on every tide. Political in-fighting was rife, envy and jealousy abounded, some interested individuals changed sides as the bidding groups jockeyed for supremacy, others kept their options open and a fascinated public watched a soccer soap opera that simply ran and ran.

Aston Villa's many history books contain stories about the great names of the past, men like George Ramsay, Archie Hunter, William McGregor, Frederick Rinder. No such individual had emerged in modern times, but one was needed now as never before, a different animal entirely from the dignitaries of a gentler past.

For Aston Villa to equip itself for the second half of the twentieth century and to be ready for the millennium a stubborn, single-minded, get-his-own-way, hands-on chief executive was required. The club's new chairman would need a grasp of the business opportunities available as modern technology and a new prosperity moved in, a man with the staying power to run and run.

In a touch of delicious irony the key to it all was to be a powerful individual with not the slightest interest in football, the cockney son of an East-End cabinetmaker. Pat Matthews was a 46-year-old multimillionaire managing director of the First National Finance Company which had been built up from the assets of the old Birmingham Railway Carriage and Wagon Company of Smethwick.

Among a group of companies he controlled was a subsidiary called Birmingham Industrial Trust, plus interests in merchant banking which gave him a profound knowledge of company recapitalisation and share flotation. To him went the job of pricing and purchasing shares from the existing directors, selling them on to their successors and organising an issue of new shares.

In the course of this process he interviewed all those parties who wished to be involved in the restructuring of Aston Villa Football Club Ltd. And he had to select well. The penalties for getting it wrong would be too dire to contemplate.

PROLOGUE

There was a spent-force board ready to move out, a slightly bewildering selection ready to move in, a balance sheet that didn't balance, a stadium that was falling apart, a losing team of questionable ability and a dwindling support. All this, remember, in the tender care of a Cockney who had seen just one football match in his entire life, though he was later to become club president.

Into this scenario of possible disaster strode one Herbert Douglas Ellis, travel agent, tour operator, one of the modern breed of entrepreneur and self-made millionaire, a restless go-getter and director of Aston Villa's greatest rivals, Birmingham City FC.

A devil's brew or the makings of a miracle? This is Doug Ellis's story.

Chapter One

U-Turn From Disaster

From Spaghetti Junction, heading towards Birmingham, make a few turns of the steering wheel, take another right past Aston Church, and ahead looms Villa Park, home of Aston Villa plc. My second home...

This almost-daily experience of arriving there, the sensation even, is always the same. Villa Park is not merely a place of work, a £126m public company, an office block with a football pitch. Yes, it is all those things, but beyond them it is a uniquely-special place to me in a way that no words of mine could adequately express.

Lifetime supporters know what I mean. They share a similar emotion when the stadium appears in view before a match. There is always a sense that something special could be about to happen.

For winter night games, especially, with the floodlights providing a halo effect, arriving at Villa Park gives the impression of a giant, outdoor theatre. Over the years we've seen many a drama played out there, that's for sure. In the last thirty years countless millions have been spent on transporting the stadium, and the entire football club, from Victoriana to the demands of the next century.

European football nights have a charisma all of their own with an atmosphere of expectancy that only devout football followers experience. To be back in the UEFA Cup in 1998-99, after the kind of season previously experienced is a rare and unexpected pleasure given that early in the year we looked far more likely to be relegated.

Even merely arriving at the ground for a normal day's work never fails to provide me with what politicians would call 'the feel-good factor'. The general impression is of everywhere being smart and ship-shape. No effort or expense has been spared as the season-by-season improvements have been completed.

Always there seems a buzz of activity in the air, particularly when preparations for a match are underway. Maintenance staff are going about their business. Members of the public are calling at the main office, the ticket office, or the Villa Village on the far side of the car park. Over there stands a souvenir shop exuding the ambiance of a top city centre store.

From it emerges a succession of fans of all ages, often clad in club replica kits. Grandma, in her own fantasy, is just as likely to be our Number 9 as some spindly-legged, two-foot-nothing toddler who might fancy his or her chances in goal.

Way back in the mists of three decades earlier my aim was to be the people's chairman of the people's club. When I see fans of all ages, both sexes, and from all walks of life togged up in our merchandise and purchasing their season tickets I presume to hope that maybe, just maybe, some may feel the ambition has been achieved.

At the main Villa Park reception desk we exchange greetings, likewise with office staff going about their business. My personal assistant, Marion Stringer and secretary, Sharon Barnhurst are busily looking after affairs in my outer office. Through there to my office where I usually remain long after normal office hours.

By now there is daily post to be dealt with, cheques to be signed, covered by a healthy bank balance, meetings to attend, immediate decisions to be made, all the daily cut and thrust of the job that I shall always enjoy. Football club finances are increasingly a topic of debate as escalating overheads eat into the admittedly high level of income. We have all read newspaper headlines of young players wanting £50,000 per week to sign new contracts, an indication of the enormous pressures placed on major clubs in pursuit of honours. The point I make here is that whilst Aston Villa would not, in the foreseeable future, bow to such demands this is the kind of world in which we compete, having once been operating whilst arguably insolvent.

Spending more than one earns can be a great temptation in any walk of life, but it will never happen at Aston Villa plc, not whilst I remain chairman. I make no apologies for being a six-days-a-week, hands-on chief executive with sensible, prudent housekeeping of primary concern.

Not a single cheque leaves Villa Park without my personal signature on it. Each day, a tray-full of invoices and their appropriate cheques arrive on my desk. Signing them all can sometimes be a painful process, but it is rather like a footballer keeping his eye on the ball at necessary moments. Administering the affairs of a major Premiership club like ours is a full-time occupation, and more, for people experienced in dealing with vast amounts of money and not afraid of the enormity of the operation.

When I study costs as they stand in 1998 I can't help but mentally compare them with 1968, when I first studied the books. Players' wages, alone now tot up to £34,000 per day! Stadium maintenance adds up to £3,250 per day, youth development costs us £1,250 and rates, water, electric and gas, a combined £1,250. Our total daily commitment works out at about £55,000.

You could have bought a half-decent player for that thirty years ago. Now the top players are looking at such sums for their fortnightly wages and, in the last four to five years our turnover in transfer fees has been around £90m.

When dealing with such astronomical figures the process of being in daily touch with income and expenditure can prevent financial own goals being scored. I can, and frequently do, pick up my internal telephone, dial our chief accountant, Phil Longmore, and ask for an up-to-date balance on the club's deposit account. His reply, this very day, was 'Sixteen point two million pounds.'

If that sounds like the prize from a roll-over lottery jackpot, then I can only say that every penny of it is needed for team building and the ground expansion plans that go on unceasingly, not to mention stage payments of transfer fees. Any day now one of the cheques will be made out for three million pounds, payee 'Liverpool Football Club' and that will complete the fee for one player, the £7m we agreed a year ago for Stan Collymore when we handed over a down payment of £4m.

Thus, the figure in our account varies, naturally, but the principle does not: Aston Villa's affairs will remain healthy because it is the only way I know to run any business. The one time in my life when I might have borrowed money was when I was first setting out on my own, of which more later, and the bank granted me an overdraft facility of £2,500. That figure remained intact. I never touched it.

'Generate income before you spend it' is my business motto, though it is pertinent, in striking a balance to draw attention to the help Aston Villa

15

gives to as many as a hundred charities and good causes each year, those in our own community as much as possible, under the umbrella of our own Charitable Trust.

These include, for example, a project with the Variety Club of Great Britain, to supply electric wheelchairs for disabled children. They were accepted at Villa Park and driven around the track by the delighted recipients. We distribute many thousands of pounds a year to those who need it. Football does put an awful lot back into its local community, most of it going unnoticed, though some examples are of a higher profile, like when we took with us several skips packed with aid to an orphanage in Romania when we played Steaua Bucharest in the UEFA Cup.

Several years before, when those deeply depressing pictures of the starving souls in Ethiopia tore at our heartstrings, we decided to charter an aircraft and despatch some Villa-aid. A 707 cargo aircraft was located in Holland and flown to Birmingham airport at a hire charge of £40,000. The sum was covered by enlisting support from here and there, while appealing to major companies to chip in with foodstuffs and medicines. At the airport our players packed the goods into the aircraft which was flown out to relieve just a little of the malnutrition, pain and suffering of these unfortunate people.

On that occasion the Blue Peter programme took up the project to illustrate that football is not immune to the needs of the less fortunate. Valerie Singleton, her TV crew and the local military were screened in Ethiopia moving the cargo up-country and supervising distribution to those who most needed it, the starving children.

We do strive to maintain this balance of bankrolling a wage bill for highly paid professionals whilst also thinking of the underprivileged.

Match days at Villa Park are always used to put something back into the public domain before the match overwhelms all else and captures our attention for whatever emotions are to be stirred this time, most of them probably. My commercial and promotional staff have me dodging around in the hour or so before each kick-off, not to mention frequently throughout every week, meeting a most fascinating range of people, mostly with a charity background. I tend to regard this as a 'perk' of the job rather than a chore.

I well recall a ninety-year-old lady season ticket holder who was mugged in her own home and her handbag stolen. "Have they taken my season ticket?" was, bless her heart, her first question. When staff heard of her wretched experience she was invited to join the directors for a special day and I was delighted to greet her. Another elderly lady, only a couple of days off her hundredth birthday also joined us for a match, and, it transpired, her father had been a Villa vice-chairman around the turn of the century. A lovely link with Villa's great past.

Such visitors love the chance to mingle with the likes of Nigel Kennedy, Jasper Carrott, John Major, maybe, and a whole host of top football personalities, past and present. The mix can be a remarkable cross-section of society.

Frequently at matches I am introduced to young people, who for one reason or another, have been invited as guests, often to take part in penalty shoot-outs or small-sided matches on the pitch for occasions they will not forget as long as they live.

For a while we actually ran a school classroom at Villa Park where local schools could bring pupils to carry out various subjects using football as a base, including getting to know the country they live in by locating all of the various football clubs, down to learning mathematics via the pitch dimensions or whatever else. Scores of schools and hundreds of children took advantage of that particular opportunity.

Our football in the community and its liaison officer, Ron Wylie, a former outstanding player and assistant manager of the club, conducts fun-coaching sessions in local schools and youth clubs on a daily and weekly basis throughout the entire year. When the holidays come Ron and his coaches run five-day courses for the children, of all ethnic groups, to keep them off the street and away from the petty crime and drug culture that is becoming an increasing problem for parents.

In the six years since Ron took over the job, now with three fully qualified coaches, I guess some seventy five thousand kids have benefited from their help in enjoying their football. Some twelve thousand individual youngsters a year, many of them more than once. In isolation some of the illustrations I have given are fairly small, the object in making them is to show that Aston Villa, with its comprehensive range of activities plays a crucial role in serving the community as a whole.

Another incalculable transformation that has taken place during the thirty years is the match-day operation on the hospitality and catering side. The normal full-time staff of a hundred and eighty, spread across all the various departments, not to mention some fifty-five players, is supplemented by eight hundred and fifty part-timers and, in an operation that would make the catering staff of a cruise-liner blanch, we serve two thousand seven hundred three-course match-day meals in our five restaurants, banqueting suite and ninety-five private boxes. Everywhere one ventures around the stadium there is the unspoken but unmistakable message that, whatever lies ahead, Aston Villa is up to the challenge. But it wasn't always like that, not way back when first I drove into the club car park to take a look at what lay behind the scenes.

The transformation between Aston Villa FC, December 1968 and Aston Villa Plc, 1998, is as far reaching as the change that has taken place in the entire face of football in the intervening years and my purpose in writing this book is to set out, in fine detail for the first time, my own part in these changes, in order to set the record straight and as, hopefully, a contribution towards the club's history for future generations.

To set this contribution, whatever the public at large judge it to be, against the background of my life as it has unfolded, rather than merely within the confines of football, I have to start with my own early years, half a lifetime before the so-called Board Revolution which, at the time of writing, is approaching its thirtieth anniversary.

Like everyone else's life, my formative years included episodes that I shall never forget.

Although, basically, I came from humble, post-World War I village life I would admit to my fair share of good fortune, like the time during the early days of World War II when I was forced to miss a boat that was subsequently sunk in the North Atlantic with all hands lost.

But for that narrow survival I would not, years later, have been able to take the helm at Villa Park when the club was firmly 'on the rocks' and also very near to going down.

Before and after these episodes life has blessed me with a kaleidoscope of memories ranging between building a business empire around the travel industry and getting the opportunity to help salvage one of the world's most famous football clubs, before steering it towards far more stable financial waters. If this sounds boastful let me stress that I see no reason in being coy about factual progress any more than I will deny my mistakes, and I've made a few, as will be shown by the events I set out to describe as accurately as memory and research allows.

I began my life in a poor, working-class family, lost my father when I was three years old, later left the Fleet Air Arm after four years war service, mostly in the Far East with only a £300 gratuity and was a millionaire before I was forty. Now, here I am in my seventies, finding myself to be the proud if rather amused possessor of a Doctorate at the University of Central England and a 'deadly' reputation for sacking football managers, though whether such a reputation is justified by the facts rather than media interpretation of those facts, will be up to the reader to judge. Just as an aside here I can quote the example of when Brian Little took me completely by surprise in tendering his resignation on the afternoon of Tuesday February 24th 1998, one national newspaper quoted eleven managers over whom I had 'presided', giving the impression that I had fired them all.

Indeed, I had not. The first one of these, Arthur Cox, was only in temporary charge before I became chairman, another, Ron Saunders, left the club when I was not there, another, Graham Taylor, left to become England manager while, whatever else may have been said or written about Brian Little's departure, the fact is that he unexpectedly tendered his resignation, quite outside of my wishes, and left the club under no pressure to do so from myself. See what I mean about exaggeration?

However, how did I become involved in this chain of events in the first place? In a way it was inevitable that I would do so. Business and football have dominated my life for as long as I can remember, so I guess it was natural that these two pursuits should join forces. This first happened in a practical sense on Tuesday December 17th, 1968. We all know the well-worn cliché about remembering where we were when President John Kennedy was assassinated or when the Birmingham bombs went off. I remember just as vividly driving down the famous Carriage Drive at Villa Park on that wintry day, my first as a director and chairman-elect of Aston Villa Football Club. What I found there provided guidelines for the rest of my life in football. One of them is that when football managers try to interfere with the business side of football clubs they are stepping out of their depth and making a big mistake.

No football manager, whose professional life has been spent on the training ground and the playing pitch would have been prepared for the immense financial balancing act required at Aston Villa FC Ltd, at that critical time following years of neglect and decline. Not a Terry Venables, not a Gordon Taylor, not a Lawrie McMenemy, nor an 'old-fashioned' director with roots too far in the past.

Thus, my first lesson was: let modern businessmen run the business and football experts run the football, a concept I have put into practice ever since. However, I digress. Back to Villa Park, December 1968... I knew things were in a pretty bad way, otherwise I would not have been appointed the previous day to launch an immediate rescue operation. Aston Villa FC was known to be dying on its feet. One of the best-known names in world football, an institution, was as near to being bankrupt as makes no matter. The former board of directors had finally given way to financial forces plus the sheer weight of public and local press opinion.

Look at the stadium today, as the year 2,000 approaches and you see one of the finest in Europe. Back then the Birmingham City fans joked that if visitors asked a bus conductor for the Hall of Memory they were taken to Villa Park. To be blunt the club had become a joke in many eyes and the challenge to all of us involved was to give Aston Villa FC a present and a future to add to the fine traditions of yesteryear. As a travel agent my motto was always that first impressions are all-important because they stay in the mind of the observer.

At Villa Park, I quickly discovered that 'first impressions' meant an antiquated front office, now long since knocked down, where a serving hatch masqueraded as a reception desk. In answer to my knock, the trap door slid open and a face appeared to ask: "Yes?".

Not "good morning" mark you. Not "how can I help you?". Just "Yes?". I was immediately appalled that this was how callers were greeted. Maybe it said it all about what lay behind that crude serving hatch.

The whole atmosphere was more like that of an old-fashioned, out-in-the-sticks railway station than of a big city football club. I know a little bit about that, as I will explain later.

On closer inspection, after climbing an old staircase, impressions did not improve. Quite the reverse. When I was taken on my first tour of the decrepit, neglected inside of the stadium it was a sad experience, indeed. Time had stood still for years on end. You could write your name in the dust. Window frames were rotting, large areas of what should have been valuable space were unused and in decay, the smell of failure and imminent financial ruin was in the air.

Long, bare corridors had paint peeling from walls, doors had cracked windows in them, bare light bulbs were commonplace. We've all seen the old Western films where the lone rider arrives in a ghost town with cobwebs and creaking doors hanging off their hinges. It was rather like that scenario. When I opened the door of the directors guests' tea room, the doorknob came off in my hand. I especially recall the so-called press room with an old-fashioned gas-fire and upright telephones with the separate ear piece on a hook.

No wonder the club was getting an unsympathetic press...

There was just one item, in the old boardroom, that I made sure to keep. This was the handsome, large, solid table. The magnificent piece of furniture was subsequently refurbished and is still in use today. If tables could talk this one would have a few tales to tell, believe me. Perusing the accounts was even worse than touring the ground. Total assets of the club including stadium, land, staff houses, and so on, was £203,770. The club's share capital was £10,000.

More significantly, the overdraft had gone through the roof, the bank manager was calling it in, the last home gate, against Charlton in the old Second Division, was a mere 12,747, relegation was looming and the playing staff was, well let's just say 'inadequate'.

What's more, the backlog of unpaid bills was quite unbelievable, the capacity to pay them was less than nil with resources haemorrhaging at an alarming rate and debts heading past a then disastrous £20,000.

In retrospect I realise now that, when I saw the true state of disrepair around the ground, the apathy among staff who had borne the brunt of the post-war slump, and the insolvency of the accounts, for all my worldliness in life and in business, I was naive and inexperienced in the daunting scale of this perilous situation.

Although I had been an Aston Villa season ticket holder for many years, had almost become a director three years earlier and had followed the decline via the press, I was unprepared for the chaotic mess that landed in our lap.

If Aston Villa were to undertake a U-turn away from disaster, things had to change, and change very quickly. This would not be achieved as, maybe, the dreamers imagined, by a snap of the fingers or a quick chat with the bank manager. In those days there was an unrealistic attitude that clubs in such a state, and Villa were not alone, had merely to appoint what was commonly known in the press as a 'Mr Big' with pots of money, who would wave a wand and all would be well.

Reality was very different and the most urgent priority was to stage our first board meeting, with two directors from the old board to give legal continuation of the company, namely Bob Mackay and Roy Ladbrooke, together with two new directors whom I had invited onto the board, Harry Kartz and Harry Parkes.

Then we would set in motion some hard-headed business methods and appoint a new manager to replace Tommy Cummings who had been dismissed by the old board before the changes, with Arthur Cox in temporary charge.

A few days earlier, having been approached by the club President, Sir Theodore Pritchett, to ascertain my willingness to consider becoming chairman, I had met up with the merchant banker, Pat Matthews, who had been appointed to organise the refinancing of the club and to select new directors who were prepared to invest £25,000 each for 5,000 shares at £5 each.

That meeting was another of those never-to-be-forgotten occasions that I will remember until the day I die. After lengthy and detailed talks at his London office we shook hands on my appointment as a director and chairman-to-be when he pressed a button on his desk. This activated a hidden door in the panelling of his office, like the entrance to some secret corridor, and from the opening stepped a smiling Tommy Docherty.

To say I was stunned would be putting it mildly. From my three-and-a-half years as a director of Birmingham City I knew Doc and was naturally aware of his chequered managerial career.

"Hello, Tommy", I said. "What are you doing here?", while thinking 'heck, he's not a new director as well, is he?' Before he could answer, Pat Matthews replied: "He's your new manager..."

New manager? For heaven's sake, I wasn't even chairman yet, not until it was formally rubber-stamped at a board meeting in accordance with the club's Articles of Association.

"Oh no he's not", I replied. "Pat, we had better get one thing straight from the start. I'll appoint the manager and if it's to be Tommy Docherty he and I have a lot of talking to do." To be sensible about it the Doc would be a good choice, bearing in mind his capacity to stir up the players, the crowd and the press.

On one hand I resented the thought of a manager being selected before I had even considered the situation but, realistically, his immediate availability to take the helm on the playing side was another point in his favour. If he were to become the first of the ten managers I have appointed, up to and including John Gregory then lines of decision-making had to be drawn up. Tommy Docherty was, in fact, appointed manager the day after I became chairman.

By now there was a subtle change. He had NOT been appointed by Pat

Matthews. He was appointed by myself and the other directors and it was to us that he was answerable.

One of the strict guidelines I put down with Tommy was that he would live, for a while, at my home where I could see and hear what was going on. The club had no resources for any spending sprees, nor was I in any position, as virtually a trainee chairman, to risk letting his natural exuberance run away with him.

The Doc had a media reputation as being something of a free spirit, an impulsive individual who sometimes acted before he thought. I wanted to make sure we BOTH thought before HE acted.

The flotation organised by Pat Matthews comprised an issue of new five pound shares and the upgrading of the original shares to 'special shares' carrying 15 votes each. A cash injection of £205,835 was raised by the flotation, less than was hoped, but nonetheless a lifeline sum compared to the total annual turnover to June 1968 of £150,720. To supplement our working capital we later appealed for those who could not afford a £5 share to make a voluntary £1 donation and this raised a further useful couple of thousand pounds.

This was the situation undertaken by Doc as manager and myself as chairman as a slightly bemused, but relieved public watched our every move. I believed then and I believe even more so now that the chairman-manager relationship has to be very close, both pulling in the same direction. That same principle applied to a degree on the board of directors. I wanted no time to be wasted on personality clashes or destructive 'splits' on the board. I had suffered quite enough of that as a director of Birmingham City for three and a half years. No way would I put up with it when I was chairman of Aston Villa.

One of my greatest strengths when I sat at the first Villa Park board meeting as chairman was that I had learned exactly how NOT to run a football club while at St Andrew's.

Blues had taught me the wrong way. I wasn't to know it then but ahead of me lay many years of battling to put into practice at Villa Park what I firmly believed to be the right way. Contrary to popular belief at that time, Aston Villa actually benefited from my experiences at the 'other' club, even though some insisted on calling me a turncoat. It was a cross I had to bear but it wasn't always easy. What I obviously couldn't say then, in the explosive climate of the time, was that I had learned about disharmony at Blues but not a lot else.

I would not be happy at Villa Park until I had an administration that was unified on important decisions and single-minded in putting them into practice. The irony of the 'turncoat' claim, however, was that I had actually become more and more an Aston Villa supporter from my first arrival in the city on April 5th, 1948. That affinity grew even stronger around Christmas 1958 when one of my old heroes from Merseyside, Joe Mercer, who a few years earlier had attended the same school as myself in Ellesmere Port, became Villa's manager.

As a Villa fan I had purchased three season tickets for Villa Park soon after I arrived in the city. Alongside them, since I was a football enthusiast, I had also purchased a Birmingham City season ticket. I liked to go to a match every Saturday afternoon. I had a couple of shares in each club, too. But for an earlier Villa Park rejection, which to this day I have never quite understood, I would have become a director at the club three-and-a-half years before, with never a thought of joining Birmingham City. Let me explain. In 1964 an approach came to me from Bruce Normansell, son of the former Villa chairman, the late Fred Normansell, a well-known fish merchant in a very big way in Birmingham, and another Villa director, Joe Heath.

Bruce, who like myself was a wartime Royal Navy man, had recognised that new blood was needed on the Villa board and that modern business thinking needed to be injected before it was too late.

Having established that I was prepared to purchase a quantity of shares, not lesser than any other director, the chairman of the day, Chris Buckley, and his colleagues invited me along to the club on the evening of a board meeting, indicating that I would be formally accepted.

Why attend the meeting, otherwise? I was met by Bruce and shown into a large, rather bare, not very warm room and asked to wait until I was summoned. I waited. And waited. Noted the dust on the shelf. Listened to the clock ticking. Gazed into space. And waited... I discovered that one director, Bill Lovsey, was on duty away from home with the reserve team and we were waiting for him to return.

Eventually, a rather flustered and embarrassed-looking Bruce Normansell emerged to say that there was a problem. The Villa board operated on a unanimous decision basis. Unless everyone agreed, things didn't happen. In my case, four of the directors had voted me in. The fifth had put up a 'black ball'. Unless he changed his mind, no Villa board place for Doug Ellis.

One of the ironies of it all was that I found the Villa directors of that era to be extremely dignified and courteous gentlemen who upheld many of the grand old club's finest traditions of honesty and old-world charm. Unfortunately their football club was going nowhere.

Chris Buckley, a former player, was the brother of Major Frank Buckley, the famous pre-war Wolverhampton Wanderers manager who introduced Stan Cullis to the game as a teenager.

Then there were men like Norman L. Smith, from the Birmingham City Council, later to become chairman, Bill Lovsey, a solicitor to a property company, Joe Heath and George Robinson, local businessmen.

In retrospect, it is probably true to say that I would not have blended with these gentlemen any more comfortably than I was subsequently to integrate with their counterparts at St Andrew's. For one thing, I was in more of a hurry to get things done than they were...

However, the day after I had attended Villa Park a very apologetic Bruce Normansell had to confirm the fact that his attempt to offer me a board place had failed.

"But why?" I asked. "What have I done except agree to put in £30,000?" That would have been a considerable investment in those days, equal to the biggest by any director of that period, which was Joe Heath's £30,000.

Bruce's answer, on behalf of the 'black ball' director was, in my mind, a classic.

In the dissenter's opinion, "I could not do anything for Aston Villa that was not already being done..." Heaven help me, had that been true, bearing in mind that all the club appeared to be doing at that time was to slide towards oblivion. I was puzzled. Disappointed. Hurt, even. I heard it said that the director concerned was 'afraid' of the new face. I have no idea if that were true.

Yet, as it transpired, events were to take an unexpected turn a few days later. I received a telephone call from the late Len Morris, a Birmingham City director whose brother, Harry, was the chairman.

"I've heard that Aston Villa have not offered you a board place," he said. How quickly the football grapevine does spread the news...

"Why not come to us, instead?" My first reaction was a completely negative one since I strongly regarded Aston Villa as 'my' club and the door had been left ajar for me to be considered again after the World Cup matches at Villa Park in 1966, when Chris Buckley would retire and create a vacancy.

Thus, any chance of my joining Birmingham City would have ended there had Len Morris not been so persistent. He pressed me to have an informal drink and snack with his brother Harry and himself at a pub, not far from the then head office of Morris and Jacombs builders.

There I was assured that a welcome mat awaited me at St Andrew's and I was invited to meet the board a few days later, having also been taken to a Birmingham match at Derby by David and Jack Wiseman. Still protesting my extreme reservations I saw no harm in going along there. The Birmingham board room was located at the time in what is now the Trevor Francis suite and before that was the D-Club.

Unlike when at Villa Park I was anticipating no more than a chat with directors but, instead, I was greeted by the chairman, Harry Morris, with his hand outstretched saying: "Welcome to the Birmingham City board, Doug. You have been unanimously accepted." How contrary life can be! At one club I've been expecting a directorship and found myself black-balled. At the other I became a director without even being offered the chance to decline.

My new board colleagues comprised Harry and Len Morris, David and Jack Wiseman, plumbers and builders, Harry Dare, a builder in a very big way, Bill Dare who was a brewer, and the former Birmingham Lord Mayor, Neville Bosworth, a solicitor and near-neighbour of mine, who later became Sir Neville.

Little did I know the extent of the politics into which I had been drawn. Another millionaire Birmingham businessman, Clifford Coombs, owner of a large credit drapery store, had previously loaned the club £80,000 but had not been able to acquire a directorship.

My arrival, it seemed, prompted the giant Welshman to demand either a return of his very significant loan or a directorship. The outcome was that Clifford Coombs, who had two sons Derek and Keith, took over as chairman. Without going too deeply into my spell at St Andrew's, suffice it to say that I found that the various families pulled in different directions and board meetings usually ended with no measure of agreement on key issues. The club didn't even have a youth team coach.

The first time I went to the Elmdon training ground there were young players like Garry Pendrey and others who were to become well-known names, just kicking a ball about on their own. I put on a track suit and joined in. I do recall once, when I was attempting to get some scheme or another through, that I was told by one of the other directors to leave football alone and stick to being a travel agent. I found that a bit rich, coming from a builder.

The one person I did learn from was Stan Cullis, the manager at that time. Stan used to ask me to travel around with him looking at players, a job that was right up my street.

Stan enjoyed being chauffeured around in my Rolls Royce, while I enjoyed going to matches with him and watching the extent Stan and his chief scout, Don Dorman, went to in checking out a player's character and lifestyle.

I well recall once that Stan was told that a particular player he was keen to sign had been witnessed going out to the pictures with his landlady, sitting in the back row, and switching on the lights in only one bedroom upon their return. Stan was aghast. Even in the so-called Swinging Sixties Stan was not going to sign a young player who might just have shared a bedroom with his landlady.

Another thing I remember about Stan: he seemed to know the best fish and chip shop on the route back from any ground in the UK. Sometimes we would divert about ten miles to get there and when we arrived scouts from other clubs would be sitting outside eating their supper from an open newspaper... a valuable part of my footballing education, I guess.

After three-and-a-half years, though, not a lot had happened, despite the board changes, to undermine my true allegiances which were claret-and-blue, not royal blue and white.

When Pat Matthews approached me to consider playing a part in the newly reconstructed Aston Villa, this time with no boardroom 'black ball' possible, I was more than happy to be transferred from Small Heath to Aston.

In any organisation or family, firm direction has to come from the top with everyone pulling in the same direction. I hadn't seen much of that at Birmingham City FC of thirty-odd years ago.

Chapter Two

Learning The Hard Way

By the time I took over the role of Aston Villa's chairman my various business activities, of which more later, were in a very healthy state. Had that not been the case I could not have thrown myself, body and soul, into the prodigious job of rescuing the club from insolvency.

Let me say from the start that I savoured every single moment of the all-consuming challenge. That's the way my life had always been. Long working hours have never bothered me. I don't even know what short working hours are.

Some are born with silver spoons in their mouths. Maybe, in a funny sort of way, I was luckier than that. I was born January 3rd 1924, with two wonderful parents who could never have afforded a silver spoon. We lived in the village of Hooton, on the Wirral mid-way between Chester and Birkenhead. My father Herbert was one of the men who returned from the trenches in the First World War, his health wrecked by gas attacks and all the other horrors they had encountered.

I have always regarded my natural instinct for 'good housekeeping' as coming from Cheshire farming stock. My mother Jane's family were farmers and while grandfather's family were also farmers, my father had completed an articled apprenticeship as a motor mechanic.

I've been told that, at age of 19, he was the first young man from Hooton to respond to the call that 'Your Country Needs You' in 1914. They also say that he was the first man to march back to the village, wearing a battle-scarred uniform and with French mud still on his puttees.

Nine years later, at the tender age of 27, he died, having earlier married my mother and set about starting his own garage business in the village to earn a living in difficult post-World War I England, and to bring up his family. The gassing he had received left him unable to fight back when he suffered an attack of pneumonia and pleurisy. The business premises near Hooton station where my father got underway with his garage, a couple of years before he died, is still there today, though when the embryo little business was broken up after his death, and sold, my mother was left with nothing.

I was three years old when he died and my baby sister Doreen was only eight weeks. Like other ladies of that era, when a generation of menfolk was ravaged by what was known as the Great War, my mother had no alternative but to get on with her life as best she could and bring up her two children with all the love and dedication she could muster, which was plenty. There was little or no welfare state to ease hardship as there is today.

Obviously, I have no personal recollections of my father, though I do have an old-fashioned, bromide photograph of him showing me how to kick a ball not long before he died.

He was a keen footballer who had been on Tranmere's books. One of my most touching moments in later years was when, having a trial at Tranmere, the club's kit man pulled out a picture of Herbert Ellis, my dad.

Although a good footballer, he was, I have been told, better known locally as a promising athlete. I do remember the small, rented semi-detached house we lived in contained many awards for his sprinting feats up to schools, county and inter-county level in the North-West.

Hopefully I have inherited some of his qualities, but the fact is that I was brought up by my mother who has had a tremendous influence on my entire life. As a widow with little or no income and two young children to support my mum had to find ways of earning a living. No doubt that is how I unwittingly acquired a business sense myself.

I was very fond of my mother, who never married again, and was heartbroken when she died, in 1988, at the age of 83 in Good Hope Hospital, Sutton Coldfield. Fortunately I had long since helped her to buy and then sell the house in Hooton and move to a nice bungalow near to myself in Four Oaks.

As for my own first attempts at earning a living I believe this began when, along with my pals, I learned that the peewit's egg was regarded as a delicacy by racegoers at the Chester racecourse on the Roodee, a large park and playing field area where our school team used to play.

We used to find the eggs in open fields, as kids did in those days, and sell them to the punters, a nice little earner then. I attended the little village school at Willaston, near Hooton, and later passed an eleven-plus type examination to move to Secondary School in Chester. Even that was a big drain on my mother who used to have to find me the rail fare which she could ill-afford.

When I was twelve I got myself a milk round at the local Jones's village store-cum-dairy, earning six shillings for a seven-day week, delivering milk from 6.30 to 8am before catching the 8.25am train. Five bob of my princely wages I passed on to my mum.

Later I started going for evening classes at a school in Ellesmere Port where the headmaster was Bill Roberts, the driving force and chairman behind the English Schools FA.

Officially I was studying shorthand and typing, but at the back of my mind I wanted to catch the headmaster's eye on the football pitch and see if I was good enough to progress! I hate to admit it, but I guess I wasn't.

I had played for Chester schoolboys, and I knew that Joe Mercer and Stan Cullis had both been spotted by Bill Roberts by attending his school, but sadly I was never going to be in their exalted class so some other career would be my lot in life, not football I'm afraid.

By the time I was fourteen and preparing to leave school I was already getting into the swing of earning money, my appetite whetted, no doubt, by those peewit eggs deals. My Uncle Fred, a farmer, once said to me, "An apple well bought is half sold" and that's a lesson I have never forgotten.

Armed with my Civil Service pass I found that there was a long waiting list to actually get an opening, so I took a job on the railway when I left school which required me to pass a joint LMS-GWR exam.

Off I went to work as a booking clerk at Little Sutton station, starting at 6.30am to supply tickets to the workers travelling to Ellesmere Port. I finished at 2.30pm when I would then endeavour to make money in any other way I could think of, the odd bicycle transaction, I vaguely seem to recall. Starting life with nothing and watching my mother struggle as she did undoubtedly motivated me to pledge that I would never suffer poverty like that as I grew up. From an early age my goal was to provide her with a better standard of living, something that, thankfully, I eventually managed to do. From 1953 to 1988, a 35-year stretch, she had a far superior lifestyle than she would ever have dreamed possible in her struggling early years.

It wasn't long after starting work that I learned that while a routine booking clerk earned 12s 6d a week you could get thirty shillings as a relief clerk working unsociable hours at whichever station you were sent.

Off I would go, any old time, to Welsh Coast stations such as Rhyl, Prestatyn, Colwyn Bay and around the Wirral peninsula to Heswall, New Brighton, West Kirby, Ellesmere Port and the like.

I did those eight-hour shifts for eighteen months and enjoyed the work, largely because I was dealing with the public. It certainly stood me in good stead for what was to follow.

On November 30th, 1941, just before I was 18, and with World War II in full swing, I volunteered to join the forces, as many young men did, and found myself in the Fleet Air Arm.

A year or so before that fate had smiled on me. And saved my life...

At the age of 16, while I was doing the rounds as a booking clerk on the railway, a job came up that truly appealed to me. George Capstick, a friend of the family from nearby, was the third engineer on a Blue Star merchant vessel and he recommended me for a job as an assistant purser on its next trip to the United States.

I was interviewed in Liverpool and was accepted for the post as a chance to open up new horizons. However, as the departure date loomed I went down with a bad attack of flu, with complications. My mother would not hear of me going and what an uncannily wise decision it proved to be. The Blue Star vessel sailed from Liverpool bound for New York without the young Doug Ellis on board and in mid-North Atlantic was sunk, by U-boats, if I recall correctly, with all hands lost including our friend, 18-year-old George.

Here again we find my mother's positive influence on my life.

It is not difficult to imagine what that generation of womenfolk went through. Having either lost, or seen their husbands, boyfriends, sons scarred for life by World War I, history was about to repeat itself some twenty eight years or so on in World War II.

My mother had lost her husband through the ravages of war. Would she now lose her only son?

I went to a base near Warrington for six weeks square-bashing and then joined HMS Daedalus at Lee-on-Solent. From there I went to HMS St Vincent at Gosport and completed my training as a Leading Seaman, Electrical.

Then came the really scary part. I was sent to Burscough in Lancashire which was a new Fleet Air Arm base to prepare ship's crews to man the Russian convoys to Murmansk and, hopefully, back.

The Fleet Air Arm pilots were trained there to do what was known as 'circuits' and 'bumps' for landing on aircraft carriers. Nerve and precision were essential.

These Russian Convoy duties were recognised among the most chilling of the war. While at Burscough, as a raw 19-year-old, remember, I was constantly in contact with the survivors of these notorious voyages.

The tales they told were absolutely horrific, as were the injuries they displayed, the horrendous scars, the lost limbs, the signs of being shell-shocked or frostbitten, or both.

Their war was carried out in temperatures so cold that their breath froze and formed an icicle to the upturned collars of their topcoats. And all the time they were being dive-bombed by the notorious Junkers 88s, based on Norwegian airfields queuing up to blow them out of the water.

Mercifully my name was never included among the crews for any of those murderous voyages to Murmansk and a far more palatable posting arrived, to sunny Ceylon, or Sri Lanka as it later became.

It was there that two further significant seeds were sown towards the creation of a successful business after the war.

The first of these was the opportunity I received to put some management skills into operation. The second was in hearing servicemen, upon seeing the world outside of Britain for the first time, saying how much they would like to travel with their wives and families when hostilities were over.

If they wanted to travel I knew an ex-railway booking clerk who would help them to do so. But first, an introduction to transport.

Ashore in Ceylon I was given the responsibility by Lieutenant Canavelli, who was from Wallasey, to start our own transport section, stores division, of the Fleet Air Arm.

I was a mere acting Petty Officer at the time and along with a Petty Officer I went along to the Army and requisitioned two Austin three-ton lorries. Eighteen months later, when the Petty Officer had moved on and with myself now in charge, I had a whole fleet of vehicles and a large number of personnel of whom fifteen were white and the remainder were Singalese.

These were made up of mechanics and drivers and we transported aircraft spares and full aircraft on large Albion Tank Recovery vehicles from the harbour at Colombo to secret air bases on the island and the naval port of Trincomalee.

Eventually I got my own staff car, rarely wore a uniform and, for the last six months as the war was ending, spent much of my time at a bungalow on the beach at Mount Lavinia, near Colombo, with two Chief Petty Officers, one of whom was in charge of the NAAFI canteen.

I worked sixteen hours a day at that operation and we consumed large quantities of Scotch, just to keep the mosquitoes at bay, of course. There was so much pilfering going on that I had to virtually reside at the depot in Macullum Road, other than when I was playing football.

My demob number came up for December 1945 and Civvy Street beckoned, but I was asked to stay on in charge of the Fleet Air Arm Transport until an Admiralty civilian came out from the UK to take over my job. I wasn't sure exactly where I was heading career-wise but it wasn't back to being a railway booking clerk, that much I knew for certain when I left Ceylon in March 1946.

Also football, even had I been good enough, was a non-starter because of a serious knee injury I had sustained while playing in a naval trial match when I was in the Portsmouth area.

I'm sure I knew even then that the person I most wanted to work for was Doug Ellis. But all I had was my £300 gratuity and a demob suit.

Chapter Three

Down To Business

In recalling my tour of duty in Ceylon I omitted to mention one special part of my life: it was there that I met my first wife, a beautiful, blonde nursing sister named Audrey Slater.

There were only about 50 white women on the island at that time and I reckon that Audrey was the best looking of them all. As for myself, I won't claim to have been the best-looking guy but I did have a certain 'pulling power' in the shape of my staff car. That was a considerable attraction at a time of limited transport, believe me.

My meeting with Audrey, with whom my second wife Heidi and myself remain close friends to this day, came about through my being admitted to the St Joseph's Hospital at the area called the Galle Face in Colombo with, I believe, a mild form of malaria.

Ceylon at that time was the HQ of South-East Naval Command under the late Lord Louis Mountbatten, whose offices were in the Galle Face Hotel. Because of the tight security arrangements on the island, as I struck up a relationship with Audrey Slater, I used to have to go and sign her out of the hospital and then sign her back in again.

Back in civvy street, in 1946, we married and settled in Preston, where I took a job with Frames Travel Agency. By chance we rented a third-floor flat about a couple of hundred yards from where Tom Finney, of Preston North End, had built himself a bungalow.

He was already a famous England international footballer then, as interest in post-war football rocketed but, like me, he presumably couldn't afford to run a car at that time and sometimes we used to meet up at the local bus stop. One day he asked me how we were settled in the flat and I mentioned that, because we were top floor, rainwater was coming in through the roof where a slate was loose.

I arrived home from work one evening soon after and Audrey said to me: "You'll never believe who's been out on our roof today... Tom Finney!".

A builder and plumber by trade, this legendary footballer, who went on to play 76 times for England had got himself up on top of the three-storey building and repaired the roof, free of charge and without being asked. Tom was knighted in the New Year's Honours List of 1998, long overdue in my opinion, and not merely because he mended my roof for nothing all those years ago.

We've been mates ever since those early post-war days. He was one of the many surprise guests at my 70th birthday party. So, too, was my first wife, and they no doubt recalled that first meeting. It was a great thrill to me that Tom spoke to the 472 guests and presented me with a life-sized oil-painting.

Significantly for what was to follow later, Frames Travel of Preston handled all the travel for the Football League and it became part of my duties to deal with the Secretary of the day, Fred Howarth.

This included travel and hotel arrangements for representative matches, including their annual fixtures against the Scottish, Welsh and Irish Leagues. One thing I shall never forget is the dinner menu which they insisted upon and which never changed... soup followed by boiled fish and potatoes. It was always the same.

Such players as Stanley Matthews, Stan Mortensen, Tom Finney and the giants of the day were weaned on boiled fish.

However, I soon became disenchanted with the drop in pay I had taken from my Fleet Air Arm pay to six pounds and ten shillings a week at Frames. I told the owner of the business, Wallace Frame, that I wanted more or I would move on.

Audrey was expecting our son, Peter, who was born in 1948, and I was far too ambitious to stand still. Wallace Frame then invited me to open a second branch of the business in Birmingham (there was already one in Small Heath), so I arrived at New Street Station on Monday April 5th, 1948 and I've been an adopted Brummie ever since.

With my own part of the Frames operation now to tackle, at the age of 24, I took an empty shop at 30 Hockley Hill, next to the post office, near the library and on the edge of the Jewellery Quarter. My basic pay was only eight pounds per week but the attraction was a commission of one per cent on my branch turnover. Now there were no bounds to what I could earn provided I was prepared to put in long hours, which I did.

That little travel agency office proved to be a gold mine. I always tell people that life presents you with little windows of opportunity and that you must take them when they are open to you. Correct timing is everything, of course, and this was early post-war Britain, a time of expansion and changing social habits.

I quickly found that jewellers or their staff would come to the post office next door to send off their precious parcels and would pop into the Travel Agent to see what was on offer. 'Going abroad' was becoming in vogue and I was ready and eager to provide the means. We did a huge amount of business in the Jewellery Quarter in the late 1940s and early 1950s and, remember, one per cent of it was mine.

Soon I was running executive, champagne-style, sporting excursion trains or so-called 'De-Luxe' rail coaches with tables, a new idea, to various venues, including football, boxing and speedway.

I developed a business relationship with the famous post-war supremo of boxing promoters, Jack Solomons, and covered every major fight he staged with ringside seats included.

One very famous championship fight for which I recall arranging a trip was the World Middleweight contest between Randolph Turpin and Sugar Ray Robinson in New York.

The businessmen from the Jewellery Quarter and elsewhere would travel with us to Wembley for big football games and championship fights and for speedway matches.

To overrun my tale slightly, I later took the post of treasurer at Birmingham Speedway and got deeply involved in the sport during its boom years. We took parties to the likes of Belle Vue and Odsall stadiums when Birmingham's glamour boy and superstar of the day was Graham Warren.

Graham went on to settle in Australia but comes back to this country sometimes and was my guest at Villa Park for a match during 1996.

In his golden years at Perry Barr attendances reached around 40,000 and similar gates elsewhere.

Eventually I took the opportunity to go half-shares with the famous former Birmingham rider, Phil 'Tiger' Hart to actually run the Perry Barr track. My little office was right next to the pits, where the bikes were roaring and sending out their acrid fumes, a little uncomfortable but the pay wasn't bad! There I looked after the admin, including collecting the gate money.

The punters used to pay two-bob a head and 'Tiger' and I would leave the track, after paying the riders and all the other expenses, with a bag of silver florins to be banked on Monday morning.

Phil had also opened up a secondhand car sales business on a former bomb site in Aldridge Road. One day, I saw him sending prospective buyers off to get their hire purchase and insurance sorted out elsewhere, I said: "Eh, why don't you provide those services yourself?".

He said he daren't take the risk, so I said that I would. This led to us jointly setting up a car insurance and finance business in Kingstanding, around 1955, with a shareholding of £12,500 each.

We would advertise 'Cheaper Car Insurance than Anyone Else' and 'Cover Notes for £10'.

Business was brisk and the enterprise lasted for 20 years, making us quite a few bob each before it was eventually closed down. Phil died recently at the age of 86.

Before the speedway involvement a major development came my way, several years earlier, which had a dramatic dual-effect of breaking up both my relationship with Frames and my first marriage.

A Canadian gentleman called into my office and he proved to be a Canadian Immigration Officer. He was looking for a travel agency to feed his country's drive to attract immigrants.

A deal of £2.10s per successful applicant was on offer and so in next to no time we were offering interviews to those who wished to emigrate to Canada, from 6pm to 10pm, after normal office hours, every week-day. There would be queues stretching outside the office and down Hockley Hill. My only staff member there was an excellent young lady named Hazel Brookes. We were both working something like a thirteen hour day throughout the week.

Within a year or two I was earning around £30 a week, a lot of money then, higher than any of the other Frames branch managers and more even than the General Manager. This caused some annoyance among the others and a meeting was called by Wallace Frame at which the threshold for earning commission was raised, reducing my income by about a tenner a week.

I wasn't standing for that, so I left Frames, taking the Canadian Immigration contract with me, since I was the one with whom they had always dealt. They wished to carry on that way and I wasn't arguing.

An empty office in Cannon Street, near the old Birmingham Post & Mail building and the Windsor public house, proved ideal. Ellis Travel Agency was duly launched on a grand outlay of £2,500.

Once established as a travel agent in my own right, with minimal capital on which to draw, the more difficult process was in obtaining the various necessary licences to, quite literally, spread my wings.

To obtain commissions on the sale of airline tickets an International Air Transport Association (IATA) licence is required. Believe me, they are granted neither quickly nor easily.

It actually took nine months for Ellis Travel to gain IATA recognition, nine months in which I operated without a penny commission on the tickets I was passing on to customers, though admittedly the commissions were eventually paid retrospectively once the licence was forthcoming.

Fortunately, soon after I started as branch manager of Frames, around 1949, I had become founder Midland secretary of the Association of British Travel Agents (ABTA). In those days I carried out a good deal of work for ABTA in getting the Midland-based agencies to join and all this had been solid experience for me in the travel business.

I was consequently aware of the benefits in becoming licensed also for the shipping lines. This I achieved with North Atlantic (which included Canadian Pacific and Cunard) and with South-East for such as P&O, Union Castle and British India.

Whilst at Frames I had enabled them to become the Midlands' largest agents for P&O Cruises, mainly by courtesy of the manufacturing jewellery fraternity who regarded a cruise as THE way to enjoy the fruits of their post-war affluence.

Far be it from me to draw any false or unfair conclusions from methods of payment but those jewellers did seem to pay more with the old 'white fivers' than they did with cheques or credit cards! Some days that little Hockley Hill office would be stacked with them.

Subsequently, when I started up on my own, due to the restrictions Frames had placed upon me, a lot of those jewellery dealers and manufacturers were happy to travel the little extra distance into the city centre for all of their business and holiday requirements.

Now those 'white fivers' were transferred to Ellis Travel, as business blossomed. That was Frames problem, not mine. I was far too occupied in moving forward to get involved in recriminations with my former employers about the past. The Canadian immigration contract was also going well and this, of course, included all of the travel business involved in addition to the £2.10s per head paid by the Canadian government for actually securing those immigrants.

In the first year we had helped 1,250 people to emigrate to a new life and now there exists near to Toronto a whole community based on the families we sent over in those early post-war days.

There was a company called Lucas Rotax at Scarborough Bluffs just outside Toronto which was largely staffed by our emigrants.

(Later, from 1963 to 1976 to be precise, I responded to an invitation to open an Ellis Travel branch in Toronto, largely to look after the requirements of the people I had sent out there.)

One of the conditions that arose in taking the Canadian contract was that I would cross the Atlantic myself to observe the industries offering jobs and the available accommodation. I was required to travel right across Canada for a month and this necessitated my taking two years' full holiday entitlement.

I was to spend most of my time in Ontario, but I also went to Saskatchewan, to Edmonton and to Calgary in Alberta.

Frames agreed to it and they put in a temporary manager at Hockley Hill whilst I was away but my wife, Audrey, was not in the least impressed with the idea. Subsequently, our marriage failed.

Meanwhile, expansion simply continued unchecked as holidays abroad became more and more the fashion. This, I suppose, led to one of the major turning points in my business career.

Although some ten years had passed I had never forgotten those servicemen back in the days near the end of World War II who, in seeing parts of the world they thought they would never see, vowed to return there with their families one day, and to travel to other exotic locations around the globe.

Making such complicated arrangements I knew would be beyond many of them and, in 1956, aware of the huge potential market, I introduced pioneering 'package deal' holidays abroad from the provinces. At much the same time similar services were offered by Sky Tours and Horizon in London and we had an agreement that we would not trespass on each other's territory.

In order to gain a broad customer-base I initiated an alliance with three other Midland-based travel agents, Joe Schutz of Transglobe in New Street, Birmingham, Laurie Bloxham of Dillinghams in Church Street, also in the centre of Birmingham, Arthur Godfrey with Godfreys of Coventry and Stan Banks of Winwoods in Worcester.

We were launched as Midland Air Tour Operators (MATO), with myself as managing director, and new horizons were opened up for the masses.

Instead of the old 'bucket-and-spade' holidays in places like Blackpool and Bournemouth, or a caravan in Skegness or Weston, ordinary families, many on moderate incomes, were suddenly transported to the sunshine of Majorca, Spain and elsewhere.

MATO chartered Dakotas from Derby Aviation, two flights each week, one to Perpignan, for the Costa Brava, one to Palma, Majorca.

In the early days the cost was about thirty guineas for two weeks, full-board, in the sunshine on the Med, inclusive of coach transfer from airport to hotel. When these wide-eyed travellers got there they discovered that they received hundreds of pesetas to the pound and that wine or brandy cost the equivalent of a few pence per litre.

Meals in the beach restaurants or foodstuffs in the stores were equally inexpensive and, what's more, the sun shone for about sixteen hours every day. It was a world they had previously only dreamed of in their wildest fantasies.

As those holidaymakers returned, starry-eyed, suntanned, packing duty-free booze and large Spanish dolls, they were already mentally booking up for next year.

One crucial component was that of keeping the cost down, which meant that we had to make everything at our end of the project cost-effective. Here again my mother, who now lived in Birmingham, and looked after Peter, was an enormous help.

Our catering consisted of my purchasing large hams and turkeys, some of which came from Billy Walker senior, licensee of the Malt Shovel hotel at Stonebridge, and my mother cutting the sandwiches to provide packed meals for on-flight consumption.

Chapter Four

Making A Million

In our first year of sending cut-price holidaymakers to Majorca and the Costa Brava the sandwiches, covered in wet lettuce to keep them moist and cut by my mother the night before, were delivered to the aircraft in biscuit tins prior to in-flight distribution.

We would take our own tea, coffee, milk and sugar with us and, on the way to the airport, I would stop off and purchase a supply of alcoholic drinks to sell en route, since there was no duty-free facility at Birmingham at that time.

The passengers used to be supplied with a cushion on which to rest their carton of sandwiches. Not very sophisticated I will admit but, remember, we were pioneers feeling our way and better catering was to follow as we developed.

There was, however, a far more serious problem than feeding the passengers, namely that of keeping them safe. Our chartered aircraft had to be loaded in such a way that the weight distributions met the necessary strict requirements to keep the propeller-driven Dakotas well-balanced in flight.

At that time there was no weighing equipment available to us because we couldn't afford to pay British European Airways the handling fee, so we used to take my bathroom scales with us to the check-in at what was more widely known then as 'Elmdon Airport', now Birmingham International, of course. By regulations a male traveller was calculated as weighing seventy-five kilos and a female sixty kilos. We not only had to ensure that our load did not exceed the permitted limits, but sometimes we had to split husbands and wives on the journey to help balance the plane.

I well remember that one of our regular captains was named Eric Lines and his wife, Audrey, would be the hostess. Tom Pike was another of our captains. My involvement, in addition to getting the business in the first place, was simply providing anything required at any time, including helping to hand out the sandwiches. Sometimes, for various reasons during the flight, I would disappear into the flight deck area.

On one occasion we had an Income Tax inspector travelling with us, one whom I recognised because I had booked him in at Cannon Street. He was sitting at the front of the aircraft watching everything that went on and I was busying myself around, helping out and, on this occasion, I must have disappeared into the flight deck for a considerable time.

Some time afterwards a colleague of the tax inspector, who also went on one of our trips, told me that when he got back to the office, he told them: "This guy Ellis, he books you in, brings the drinks, hands out the sandwiches, and what's more, he flies the f——-g thing as well..."

That 'slightly' exaggerated summing up confirmed that the package-deal holiday had arrived and in 1962, when I sold Sunflight, another business I had started, to Sir Isaac Wolfsen, the *Evening Mail* in Birmingham, ran a story declaring that the deal had made Doug Ellis a millionaire.

Since then I have learned that not every story you read in the press is true but, to be fair, I had no cause to deny that particular one. In 1956, without business partners, I began operating, from Manchester, a new company which I named Sunflight, with twin-engined Vikings. For the next 20-years I expanded with flights from Glasgow, Edinburgh, Belfast and Dublin. Together with MATO, which I had now bought out from my original partners, this became the largest air tour operator outside London, flying to France, Italy, Spain, Morocco, Yugoslavia and Tunisia with four-engined Viscounts, a DC4 and a DC6B.

I sold Sunflight to Sir Isaac Wolfson, chairman of Great Universal Stores, but retained MATO. By this time I also had twelve retail travel agencies in different cities throughout the UK and Canada, booking passengers by air, sea and land.

Meanwhile, in the course of constantly travelling back and forth to Majorca and Spain in connection with block bookings for the package-deal holidays I inevitably forged strong contacts with several hotels. This led, ultimately, to my having five of my own amounting to a total of 600 bedrooms which we constantly filled with our own holidaymakers.

Just outside Palma, Majorca, there was the Rosamar in Terreno, the Mar Azul in Cala Ratjada on the northern coast, which I still have, the Grand Sol in Cala Bona, the Albatross and the Clara Mar on the Costa Brava, all constantly occupied by the guests whom we had booked in at one of our offices. Alongside the travel business other interests also developed over a period of years, including farming, construction and a chain of various retail shops, notably butchers, cafes and shoes.

Ellmanton Construction was another of my companies. For years Ellmanton built leasehold dwellings around the area and though the building activities ceased a few years ago the company is still in existence and receives, via our agent Shaw Gilbert, income from the houses, shops and flats it created.

For a number of years Harry Kartz, who was also to become a Villa director and chairman, and myself jointly owned a number of racehorses which were based on my stud farm near Lichfield where we bred and raced thoroughbred horses.

At our peak in racing I owned or shared in twenty-three bloodstock, including the fine mare Julie Andrews, and the colt, Ellkar. With Tom Taylor as my private trainer at Aldershawe I persuaded a few friends to place their horses with Tom and in one outstanding season he produced nine winners, though throughout it all my main sporting love outside of football has been salmon fishing, of which more later.

During the same period, when my business policy was one of diversification, or Vertical Integration as it is termed, we also ran our own coach company for the convenience of our holidaymakers.

My purpose in dwelling on all these aspects of my business affairs is to illustrate the grounding it gave me in working to get all possible essential services supplied under your own roof, so to speak. The principle has been a main plank of our thinking at Villa Park.

With this approach one has to be constantly watching the market and being ready to meet public demand. For instance when it emerged that a trend towards self-catering holidays was developing our travel agency responded.

In order to meet this demand we built, in conjunction with a Spanish builder, our own block of self-catering apartments named Ronda in

Fuengirola, consisting of a lounge, kitchen and two or three bedrooms. When completed we had 234 apartments with 720 beds and found that Mr and Mrs Joe Public were ready to fill them. I well remember a photograph being published in the *Birmingham Mail* of our passengers setting off from the airport, armed with their kettles, all ready to make a nice English cuppa on arrival at their destination.

Shoes were another commodity that found their way into our multi-purpose organisation for a year or two when I financed, on behalf of a friend of mine, a shoe shop in Erdington. This outlet provided the opportunity to take up vacant storage capacity in the hold of our chartered aircraft to bring back supplies of highly-fashionable shoes from both Spain and Italy to be sold in the Erdington shoe shop.

When I reached the peak of my business diversification in the 1960s I also had financial interests in three butchers' shops, two cafes, an electronics factory in Nuneaton and a couple of farms, one of them for stud and bloodstock purposes.

Car hire was yet another activity in which we were involved for a while, based at 117 Grafton Street, Dublin. This was to meet the needs of American travel agencies sending tourists over to Ireland needing motor cars to get around.

We purchased a fleet of 15 Morris Minors in the late 1950s and though it proved not to be a major profit-maker it did add to our all-round services.

For a period of time in the 1960s there was also an Ellis Staff Agency Ltd with three offices in Birmingham, Dudley and Wolverhampton and this unwittingly led to my being advised by the chief constable of Birmingham, Sir Derek Capper, that I could be quite wrongly suspected of starting a very dubious business, indeed.

At that time there was a dire shortage of shorthand typists in the Midlands, so with the old maxim 'where there is a shortage, find the supply and you are in business' I set about making plans. The bizarre episode began at my office in Cannon Street, Birmingham, where we had a staff of 50 on three floors, including some 30 girls on various shorthand and typing duties. On stopping to chat to any newcomers as I passed through it came to my notice that a staff agency was being used by our department managers for recruitment purposes. The revelation didn't please me one bit. Employing staff in this way was an expensive exercise so I hit upon what I thought was an original and novel way of starting up our own agency.

I knew that, whereas in Birmingham at that time, there were more jobs than typists, in Hong Kong the reverse was the case.

Off I flew to Hong Kong where I had a hotelier friend who confirmed my belief that there would be a big response from local girls, with both the necessary qualifications and a British passport, seeking secretarial work in England. To test the theory he advertised in the local newspaper and quickly received about 200 replies. It was instantly clear that we could obtain a supply of such girls to either work in our travel agency or be offered work by Ellis Staff Agency.

Two practical problems remained. How were we to get them over here and where were they to live? Simple. Or so I thought. Another friend of mine, Harold Bamberg, who ran Eagle Aviation, had regular flights to the Far-East and readily agreed to bring girls over when he had vacant seats on return journeys.

As for the accommodation, I had an apartment block in Moseley which, at that time was virtually empty, ideal for the Staff Agency girls to reside whilst they were working over here as shorthand-typists.

Soon our plans were progressing encouragingly. We designed a smart blue uniform with nice white blouses and a split skirt, the fashion of the day, so that the girls would look the part.

My hotelier friend chose tall, elegant young ladies who would look good when we launched the agency and arrangements were in hand for the first group to arrive a few weeks hence.

I had in mind a nice picture opportunity for the press at Birmingham Airport where the girls would disembark, wearing their uniforms and line-up wing-tip to wing-tip as the pioneering recruits for Ellis Staff Agency.

When all was in hand I was chatting to Sir Derek, a regular at our Villa Park matches when he was chief constable, and asked him whether he was short of shorthand-typists at the police headquarters in Steelhouse Lane. Indeed he was. At that I proudly outlined my scheme to him and off he went looking slightly quizzical. Early on the following Monday a lady police officer rang my office to say that Sir Derek wished her to talk to me. Along she came with, to my amazement, a special request from him to abandon the idea which he reckoned was fraught with danger. "What you plan to do is not illegal," I was told. "But groups of girls living in a block of flats in Moseley will attract kerb crawlers and other unsavoury characters who assume that the girls would be available for far more lucrative services than shorthand-typing." To use a modern expression, I was gob-smacked. Such an interpretation of an innocent business initiative had never occurred to me. So, although frustrated at having what seemed a good idea denied in this way I could only accept the chief constable's advice, though my staff agency ran for some years and earned a small fortune.

Recruiting clerical staff was one thing. Being accused of taking on a team of streetwalkers was not the name of the game I wanted to be involved in at all and to be fair I didn't need any further growth in my activities!

Success in business had enabled me to purchase a villa near Palma and a boat down in the harbour to add cruising as another enjoyable pastime. Also for a time I dabbled in sports car racing, driving an Alfa Romeo, but back trouble and the awkward seating position put paid to that and a more comfortable and less adventurous Rolls Royce took over.

Basically during the 1950s and 1960s my business involvement grew and prospered in several directions including, somewhat to my surprise, as a wine dealer.

One of my closest hotel contacts in Spain came to me and asked whether I would consider taking quantities of wine from his parents who had a small vineyard in the hills and were producing far more wine than the Valencia co-operative would take from them.

This, remember, was back in the days when there was only a fraction of the demand for wine that there is today and through limited demand, all this couple's surplus was seemingly going to waste.

A deal was quickly struck with them and they were delighted to be paid the equivalent of five old pence per litre for all that Spanish Red that would otherwise presumably have disappeared down the drain.

Soon I had a bottling plant in the cellar of one of my hotels and we were able to amply supply our bars and restaurants with our own vintage.

It was not, I suppose, a Rioja to delight the expert palate, but certainly a more-than-acceptable Ellis Red to quaff and enjoy.

Some of it, you will not be surprised to read, would naturally end up at my home in Four Oaks where guests would be quite impressed to be served wine with a personalised label, which they assumed to be an expensive choice especially for the connoisseur.

I would cheerfully allow them to wax lyrical about its rich fruitiness and pleasant bouquet before informing them that my 'vintage' wine actually cost five pence a litre.

It was none the worse for that, I can assure you.

By now I was happily remarried. Having ended my marriage with Audrey in 1954 I was eventually captivated by Heidi. She was a courier with Sky Tours and a very good one at that who, among her talents, spoke English, German, Spanish and French, fluently.

It took me some eighteen months to convince the lovely Heidi that she should marry me, but marry me she did in 1963.

We had a Registry Office ceremony in Birmingham and a far grander church wedding at her parents' home near Hamburg. We have two sons: Simon, who is making a name for himself as a musician and songwriter based in Dusseldorf, and Oliver who works in TV production for an Anglia TV subsidiary as head of children's and entertainments programmes.

At the time of writing, some thirty-five years after our wedding Heidi would possibly say that I am actually married to Aston Villa Football Club. If so it would be a suggestion I could hardly deny. Certainly I would have to agree that Heidi and Villa are two loves I have fought tooth and nail to include in my life. Heaven knows how things would have worked out without her support and forbearance for which I could never thank her enough.

She was the head courier for Sky Tours based in Benidorm. A single girl, stunning to look at, she lived in a very small one-room flat which was provided by her employers. There was a boy friend in my way, as one would expect of such an attractive young lady.

From the start I was attracted to her working ability and the excellent job she did for her employers. But that wasn't all. I was also totally bewitched by her beauty and the sort of person she was. There was I, now her ardent suitor, divorced and unattached and, some ladies would no doubt have said, an eligible bachelor of considerable means. Yet, if Heidi noticed she didn't let on. I tried all I knew to get her to go out with me but to no avail. She simply kept me at arm's length. In due course I was able to persuade her to change jobs and to work for my company, rather than Sky Tours in Benidorm and in so doing was able to provide her with a nicer and more spacious flat.

Professionally, at least, I had the power to tell her what to do, but she still kept our relationship on a strictly boss-employee basis for quite a considerable time.

Younger readers will probably scoff when I use the word 'courted' but this in fact was what I had to do to win Heidi's hand in marriage even though I was based in Birmingham and she in Benidorm. The ace up my sleeve in pursuing my interest in her, quite apart from now being her boss, was in being an air tour operator.

Every week I flew abroad to somewhere or other, so I made it my business to visit Valencia as often as possible, every other week, maybe.

When I did so I would request that my head courier in Benidorm must jump into a taxi, take the two-hour journey to Valencia airport, pick me up, and transport me back to Benidorm and, the next day, return to Valencia. Those cunningly-arranged taxi drives were a winner as far as I was concerned because it meant I could mix business with pleasure and do a spot of old-fashioned 'courting' during the journey, all strictly verbally, of course, but it was a start.

This 'romantic' recipe appeared to work because she gradually agreed to go out with me socially.

One weekend, just to impress her (heavens I must have been in love!) I arranged for my brand-new Mercedes SL 190 sports coupé to be driven down to Benidorm whilst I was being flown in via Valencia. Now I was able to whisk her along the sea front in my sparkling, open-topped sports car where she could be the envy of her courier colleagues and friends, among them I hoped, her former boy friend. For a lad who used to be carted around on the back of his mum's bike as she took in washing to survive, I reckoned that wasn't bad!

When I saw how much Heidi loved the sports car I left it with her in Benidorm and, to continue the wearing-down process, I provided her with a winter job in England, based in Manchester.

Once here she was able to take part in the annual Christmas parties which I staged for staff plus those travel agents who worked on our behalf, and their wives. These functions went round five centres in turn, namely Birmingham, Manchester, Glasgow, Belfast and Dublin.

Eventually my courtship, spread over many thousands of air miles, not to mention those taxi drives, won me my bride and she became Mrs H D Ellis in March 1963. Thirty-five years on she is still Mrs Heidi Ellis and we have resided in the same house all that time.

Peter, my son from my first marriage, was a co-director of Aston Villa and has been very successful in building up the Aston Manor Brewery, into which we purchased a substantial interest after it had been founded near the site of the former Ansells Brewery, not far from Villa Park.

Peter was captain and head boy of Repton School and an outstanding young footballer. Stan Cullis saw him play in a trial match for Birmingham City when, as a young defender, one of his tackles put Bertie Auld, later to win a European Cup-winners medal with Celtic, over the touchline.

Stan offered him a professional career but, to my total frustration, bearing in mind my own unsuccessful early aspirations, he turned it down preferring to play football for fun. Peter later joined my travel business after leaving a firm of chartered accountants and subsequently became managing director of my building company, Ellmanton Construction, before taking the reins at Aston Manor Brewery Ltd where he remains as financial director.

Having recounted the Hong Kong episode I recall another experience of police intervention in my business affairs was far less amusing. 'Deeply disturbing' would be a better description, especially for Heidi. She was often, literally, on the receiving end of a distressing situation. In the early years at Villa Park, when results were not always to supporters' liking, I started to receive abusive and threatening telephone calls at my home.

Quite often it was Heidi who took the wretched, cowardly calls and as a result she twice suffered nervous breakdowns, and no wonder since the callous callers sometimes talked of kidnapping our sons.

It became so frequent and so bad that, when we had been out in the evening we would return and leave the lights off in preparing to turn in for the night. This was because a pattern was established of the calls often arriving as soon as our house lights went on. The police felt that the culprit or culprits were parked in a van nearby with walkie talkie equipment and keeping the house under surveillance prior to making the upsetting calls.

With the curse of hooliganism taking root, the verbal attacks were felt to be football, rather than business related, although another even more disturbing incident occurred during the period when the IRA pub bombings and the like were in people's minds.

My telephone rang during the early hours of the morning and as I awoke sleepily to answer it I was mumbling about the 'yobbos' being up to their tricks again. This time, however, a voice announced that it was the assistant chief constable, Harry Robinson, calling. Being dubious about its authenticity I asked for a number so that I could ring back and, sure enough, it proved to be the police office at New Street Station. The caller was, indeed, Harry Robinson.

"They've got you this time, Mr Ellis..." he said. "They've blown up the front of your premises on the station concourse." Suddenly I was wide awake.

Obviously my automatic reaction was that I would be there in half-an-hour, but he advised me to go back to bed and he would get the shop-front all boarded up until I arrived next morning. The police are accustomed to such situations but to Heidi and I it was a profound trauma. After a quick discussion we agreed with the advice and when I looked for myself next day I learned that a bomb had been placed at the door, blowing out the front of the premises and virtually wrecking the office inside.

It was an uncomfortable experience, I can tell you. No message was received from the perpetrators of the crime, nor was anyone ever apprehended. For a while afterwards I felt the need to be 'looking over my shoulder' whenever, for instance, I walked from my office at 44 Cannon Street to the Birmingham Club in Ethel Street where I would have a lunchtime snack and maybe a frame of snooker.

Heidi's nerves took a considerable time to recover from the ordeal and answering the telephone was not her favourite activity... such was one of the penalties of public life.

The bottom line to the details I have described about my upbringing and background is that by the time I became Aston Villa chairman for the first time I had learned a thing or two about sport, football in particular, financial struggle, business development, making profits, life in general and, most of all, people.

I was going to need every scrap of that experience, enthusiasm and business instinct at my disposal as the rest of the story will show.

Chapter Five

Doc's Arrival – And Departure!

Tommy Docherty was once described as being "Like a fire engine speeding to blaze after blaze with its blue lights flashing and its siren sounding non-stop".

Sure, there's a hint of journalistic over-statement in the description but it is not a bad analogy, as I was to discover. When Doc started what was to prove a fairly short, thirteen-month term as manager of Aston Villa FC he had recently completed a mere twenty-eight-day spell in a similar capacity with Queen's Park Rangers. Tommy lived his life in the headlines and the public at large waited eagerly for their newspapers to avidly read the next Villa story, and the next.

When he was appointed on Wednesday December 18th, Doc felt it was too late to take charge of events for the Saturday's home game with Norwich. He left that to the acting management team of Arthur Cox and Peter Doherty, who had been in charge since the previous manager, Tommy Cummings' dismissal.

But, as Tommy Docherty eased his way into Villa Park, all sorts of things were going on behind the scenes. I had invited ex-Birmingham *Evening Mail* writer, Eric Woodward, to return from his administrative post with Atlanta Chiefs in the North American Soccer League to be appointed as one of the game's first commercial managers and our club Public Relations Officer.

Eric was ready to return to his native Birmingham after two years of successfully helping to launch soccer in the United States along with the former Villa player, Welsh international and BSc, Phil Woosnam. I was well-aware that Eric had been out selling this 'new' game to the American public. Now he could come back and help to sell the 'new' Villa to the city of Birmingham and its surrounds.

In my first press conference I stressed that my ultimate aim was to make Villa Park a multi-purpose stadium available for a whole range of activities, 365 days a year, if feasible. "I want Aston Villa to be another Real Madrid," I announced a shade presumptuously for a club heading for the Third Division! But I meant it; Eric was going to be busy...

Also, I never tired of pointing out that working populations of major European cities rely heavily on the performance of their favourite team to provide moments of euphoria in their lives. As an example I would cite the experience in Turin where the huge Fiat work force ebbed and flowed in productivity terms depending on the fortunes of their beloved Juventus.

It was my conviction that great changes were afoot in society at large and one of these was that industry and commerce would become more closely linked to football clubs. This was the way ahead for Aston Villa, I had no doubt about that then and I've never altered my stance.

As quickly as possible I intended to have a line of executive boxes created at the front of the main Trinity Road Stand and to invite businesses to hire them on lengthy contracts.

These match-day hospitality units are commonplace now, but it was pioneering progress then and it is amusing to note that our first suggested contract was £5,000 for a ten-year lease.

Another local headline-grabber was our appeal for scores of volunteers to come along to Villa Park on Sunday mornings armed with their own paintbrushes to give the dreary, dilapidated old stadium a face-lift with a series of huge communal paint-ins. The true Villans did come along, too, bless 'em, and when we asked industry to help us by providing gallons of paint, that was forthcoming also.

Basically, we appealed to bricklayers, electricians, plumbers, carpenters, carpet-layers and the like to come along and show their concern for the club by carrying out a necessary service, free of charge.

One of the early good souls to respond to our SOS was a local builder, name of Ted Small, who subsequently became, and still is, our Stadium Manager and who has played a leading role in making the stadium what it is today. The first businesses to respond to our appeal were BIP Reinforced Products of Streetly, and Paynes of Aston, who offered to replace all the smashed windows in the Holte End on a complimentary, goodwill basis. The magnificent gesture was accepted in the spirit with which it was offered and others followed.

Part of the flotation scheme was that Birmingham Industrial Trust purchased 699 shares from the previous directors at £60 each and that 'old' shares were to become 'special shares' worth fifteen of the £5 new shares, and the equivalent number of votes. I was reminded of this by the more recent flotation in which these £5 shares had achieved a value of £1,100, making those 'special shares' increase pro-rata. Then, as more recently, searches were undertaken in Villa homes everywhere for those precious share certificates which had suddenly escalated in value.

To help us get underway Pat Matthews arranged a working overdraft of £50,000 which, even in those days meant that financially we were constantly treading a tightrope without a safety net. Generously, the resigning director, Joe Heath, having sold some of his shares to Pat Matthews, loaned £30,000 of it back to the club at a low interest rate. It helped a lot. But we were very hard up.

Those early days from the Christmas-New Year period of 1968-69 are recalled nearly thirty years on as a blur of activity, action, controversy, wisecracks and public expectation.

For that first match under the new regime, against Norwich on Saturday December 21st, 19,923 fans turned up on, remember, the worst-supported day of the season, 7,000 better than the previous match.

The public hadn't quite taken it all in and the Doc had made it clear that, on this occasion, he was just watching and learning. There was an atmosphere of expectancy in the air but, as we won 2-1, it was only the calm before the storm of hysteria which was to hit Villa Park on Boxing Day when Jimmy Scoular's Cardiff were the visitors.

To be fair to Tommy he got the whole thing off in ideal fashion by signing Brian Tiler, whom he had admired when he was manager at Rotherham before his brief stay at QPR, three days before his first game at the helm. On a sad note, Brian was tragically killed in a road accident in Italy during the 1990 World Cup.

Trying to sign Tiler from Rotherham had been the issue to cause Docherty's split with Queen's Park Rangers only three weeks earlier. According to reports Rotherham's asking price was £100,000 and Rangers' chairman Jim Gregory wouldn't agree. Doc, being the Doc, emptied his desk and left.

Whatever the truth or otherwise of that account we got Tiler, in a quick, uncomplicated deal. He was signed for around half of the original asking price to skipper a team that had long since lost its way and thus we went into those opening games of the club's new era with a new captain, new manager, new board and new chairman.

"My name is not Oliver, it's Tommy," said Doc to the local papers in typically colourful fashion before the game. "The 19,000 for Norwich was great. But please can I have some more..."

At that time Apollo 8 was making its historic first orbit of the moon and blizzards were forecast around the country for a white Christmas, but Villa Park was suddenly the only focal point for Villa fans responding to the new deal. An amazing crowd of 41,250 was at Villa Park for that Boxing Day game and Tommy Docherty and Arthur Cox were like jumping Jacks on the touchline, orchestrating the outpourings of support.

Had Doc staged-managed the whole affair there couldn't have been a more spectacular kick-start for the new Aston Villa, when, although the white Christmas didn't arrive the icy, slippery pitch was regarded by many as being 'unplayable'. The game was almost farcical but Barry Hole gave us a first-half lead and then, in the second half, a Mike Ferguson corner curled in for new man Tiler to race in, leap up and sign in with a superb headed goal that ensured our second successive victory. The roar must have been heard right across the frost-bound city.

Two days later we were at Carlisle and that fixture was to mark our volatile manager's first big controversy. Because of the weather many fixtures were off so additional spotlight was focused on our game, helped by the Doc factor.

After a rugged, battling 90 minutes on a bone-hard surface we emerged as 1-0 victors through a goal by Willie Anderson. Carlisle had previously moved up the Second Division with a 13-match unbeaten run under Bob Stokoe. To under-state the case, Bob wasn't pleased about the defeat. He reckoned that Tommy's team had been negative, obstructive and more interested in time-wasting than indulging in a free-flowing game. Bearing in mind our desperate position in the Second Division, maybe he was right.

"I would rather sweep the streets than play like that..." Bob told the larger-than-usual gathering of media at the game.

Sure enough his scathing words hit the headlines up and down the country and Doc's Villa were labelled as destroyers. To my knowledge

Tommy lost no sleep over the complaints. "Stokoe had better watch what he says or I'll report him to the FA", he coolly responded with just the follow-up the press wanted to produce more headlines the next day.

But there was an amusing sequel when next we played Carlisle, at Villa Park. Before the game the visitors' dressing room door was pushed open and a broom was tossed in by one of the Villa players, presumably to help the Carlisle manager to 'sweep the streets'.

Mr Stokoe distinctly did NOT see the joke but we had more important issues on our mind.

For instance, on my first day at the club, the eve of Tommy Docherty's appointment, I had wanted to meet the players for the first time. They proved to be at a sports ground in Cooksey Lane, where they trained as 'lodgers'.

Frustratingly the previous board had sold an ideal training ground, near to Villa Park which they had purchased and had subsequently sold, far too cheaply, for building development. Seeing our players training on a works ground reminded me of another urgent priority: we had to acquire our own facility in addition to all the other requirements.

Clearly, with so much finance required for so many projects, success on the field was an absolute must and things were off to an encouraging start.

In the first three weeks after the changes a thousand new season ticket holders were signed up, thus attracting £4,500 of new revenue.

This may sound a derisory figure all these years on, but it was quite a significant amount in those days and gave the bank manager a modicum of renewed confidence. Another £2,000 was raised by an unusual one pound bond scheme.

The 'pound bond' was suggested by Frank Owens, the editor of the Birmingham *Evening Mail* at that time, to be run through the columns of his newspaper. Each person who sent a pound received a scroll acknowledging their financial support in Aston Villa's most critical hour of need and personally signed by myself.

Around 2,000 responded. Many of the scrolls were framed and hung on walls around this country and abroad, but one reaction to the scheme sticks vividly in my memory. An airmail-type letter arrived from a location in Germany from the Burgomaster of a little town who had seen an item about our pound appeal on Eurovision.

Expressing regret that Aston Villa was in financial difficulties he went on, in broken English, to explain his most moving affinity with the club.

He had been a prisoner of war at a camp on Cannock Chase where his one pleasure during captivity had been to secretly get out and make his way to our games and back without his absence being noticed.

This he achieved every other Saturday by getting his hands on a civilian raincoat to cover his immediately-obvious POW uniform, crawling under the barbed wire and walking the 'eight or ten miles' to Villa Park and back. Obviously I cannot remember his exact words thirty years on, but they were to the effect that he thanked Aston Villa for helping him through his internment and, though not a wealthy man, he was enclosing twenty Deutchmarks towards our appeal, wishing us every success with it.

Another case of football cutting across the animosities of war and political strife to create lasting friendships. We gave this lovely story, as we saw it, to the *Evening Mail* and suggested that if they were to fly the ex-POW over we would give him VIP treatment at a match and they could have an exclusive picture-story to publish. They declined unless we were to pay the air fare, a trifle paltry of them we felt at the time.

By then we had made it our business to keep the local press supplied with stories every day, not too difficult a task with the volatile Tommy as manager, Eric Woodward as experienced press officer and myself as chairman. The *Mail* had done especially well, as anyone can check by digging out the files of the late 1960s early 1970s, but there were times when I felt that the spirit of co-operation was a shade one-sided.

The limited strength of the squad was a problem, as were the social habits of some of its members. Before we took over there had been Sunday paper reports of what one might call 'unprofessional behaviour' off the field, though it was Sunday School stuff compared with some of the excesses one reads of in the tabloids three decades on. let's just say that a certain player, who shall remain nameless, attracted a Holte End chant that concluded: "He's up, he's down, he's in the Rose and Crown".

To be accurate the 'Fox and Dog' in Four Oaks, not far from my home, and thus Doc's too, at that time, was the place that the many anonymous callers specified as the meeting place for Friday night drinking sessions.

One particular Friday, before a match next day, my telephone rang and a concerned supporter informed us that a group of our players were knocking back the pints of ale in the bar of the 'Fox and Dog'.

"Come on Tommy", I said. "We'll nail 'em red-handed." Off we went in my Rolls and nipped into the lounge, from where we knew you could see through the serving hatch into the bar.

Doc's Arrival – And Departure!

Sure enough our lads, the known culprits, were sitting around a table laden with pints of beer. 'We've got 'em...' we thought. However, we must have taken a little while to make our way through to the bar, maybe via the loo or whatever, because when Tommy and I walked into the bar to 'nail 'em red-handed', all you could see on the table were glasses of orange juice. How well they must have had the pub's grapevine sorted out.

There was never a dull moment with The Doc around. When there was an outbreak of hooliganism, for instance, he called for the culprits to be publicly birched. Not one for half measures, our Tom.

There was always plenty of Mickey-taking going on in those days and I have painful memories of being the victim of one incident when I unwittingly set myself up to be fall guy. The old urge to kick a football myself had not yet burned itself out and I remember on one occasion being encouraged to join in a practice match at Villa Park.

All was going OK, although I was reminded in the opening moments that professionals play a quite different game to enthusiastic amateurs, especially those of advancing years. On a rare occasion when I managed to have the ball at my feet I took a tackle on the ankle which led to my being carried off in considerable pain for attention by the physio. It was the same ankle I had injured while playing football in the Fleet Air Arm.

After treatment I went into the dressing room showers which were in different cubicles and while I was in one of them Brian Godfrey, the Welsh international, went into the adjoining one and must have assumed I had left. Amid all the banter he gave a wicked little chuckle and said in a loud voice to no-one in particular: "Did you see how I clobbered the ******* chairman?" I could only imagine how his face must have looked when I replied from 'next door': "I did, Brian. I can still feel it." There was a pregnant pause before he replied: "Sorry Mr Ellis. I didn't know you were there." Obviously...

Doc and I got on very well as relegation was avoided and we set about creating a junior scouting scheme up and down the country. On a Sunday morning, for instance, we would fly to Newcastle to see a boys' match at our nursery club and then onto Glasgow where we would watch two matches of boys in different age groups before meeting the parents over a cup of tea and a bun.

Eric Woodward was getting things like catering, the club programme, fund-raising and other commercial affairs on a businesslike footing and the club was edging away from the brink of disaster.

But, unhappily, on the field the euphoria did not last despite what we felt was a scoop in signing Bruce Rioch, along with his brother Neil, from Luton Town for £100,000 in July 1969. For us to be able to spend such an amount of money was progress in itself.

Bruce had scored 24 goals in 44 league games for the Hatters when they won the Fourth Division Championship the previous season.

The Rioch signing, at such a high fee for a club still in dire financial difficulties, sent a message around the game that we truly meant business. Oddly, it unwittingly also created intense hostility from a local newspaper editor. I recall the chain of events vividly. When our new administration moved in I told local reporters from the national and provincial press that while Aston Villa would be 'reaching for the stars' we needed each-way co-operation to bring it about.

For our part we would never withhold information in order to favour either the morning or the evening papers. News, such as transfers, would be released as soon as negotiations were completed, whatever the time of day or evening.

This point I emphasised particularly, because a number of morning newspaper journalists had privately made the point to me that the *Evening Mail* always seemed to get the information first.

Among the journalists voicing this concern was the late Alan Williams of the *Daily Express*, the late Mervyn Thomas of the *Daily Mail* and Ian Willars, then the *Birmingham Post* football correspondent. Ian later moved to the *Evening Mail* himself and on to the *Sports Argus* where, up to the time of writing, he has remained.

After I had made my pledge to the press Ian came to see me to say how much his editor, David Hopkinson, appreciated the promise of a fair crack of the whip for all.

Here, perhaps, I should explain that any news announced before around one o'clock could then get a big 'splash' coverage in that evening's main edition. The longer the afternoon progresses, however, and certainly into the evening, then stories come up nice and fresh for the morning papers. Such news releases influence sales considerably and it was felt that, prior to our arrival, there had been a 'leak' from the old Boardroom to the *Evening Mail*.

Unfortunately, however, due to pure circumstances, the process of news getting out first for the evening newspapers continued as transfers always seemed to be completed before lunch.

Doc's Arrival – And Departure!

It must be remembered here that we had as our commercial manager/PRO, Eric Woodward who was himself an ex-*Evening Mail* chief football writer.

The suspicion seemed to be growing, quite wrongly but perfectly understandably, that we were continuing to favour the evening papers. Had I, they wondered, been dishonest in my promise of fair shares for all? They could point to morning papers, including the *Birmingham Post,* still constantly being left only with 'follow-ups' to news announced the previous evening.

Proof to the contrary was required and our bid for Bruce Rioch appeared to offer me the chance to balance the books. We could give the morning papers first bite of Aston Villa's club record signing and my promise would be honoured. By three o'clock in the afternoon the deal was more or less concluded. Tommy Docherty and I set off for Luton. Tommy knew Bruce's mother quite well, and she was a major influence on the household. We simply felt that, on balance, it was better for us to be in Luton than have Bruce travel to Villa Park.

The timing seemed perfect for the *Post* although there was now a delay because Bruce's younger brother Neil, himself a promising player, had been introduced into talks for a dual signing.

By around 6.30 pm, as talks progressed, it seemed sensible to alert the *Post* to be prepared. There I made my big, big mistake in authorising that they be advised to leave their sports page headline and lead story open because, no names yet, but we had a big transfer story coming up for them. Tommy went off to the Rioch home. I remained at Kenilworth Road with their chairman. Time ticked away. The Rioch family drove a hard bargain in terms of our signing not now one, but the two footballing sons. It all took longer than we expected.

As the *Post's* deadline approached and passed negotiations were not completed. Nobody's fault. That's how it happened despite our best intentions. It was the following morning before it was all signed and sealed. In Evening paper time again.

The *Post* felt very badly let down as I quickly discovered. I had arrived home from Luton around midnight to be greeted by a person-to-person call from David Hopkinson who was then in Berlin on business.

He was distinctly NOT pleased. Judging by his aggressive and abusive manner his displeasure was inflamed by a couple of drinks. Or maybe three. 'Hoppy', as he was known by his staff, was hopping mad. He accused me of trying to wreck his newspaper. My protestations that we had been overtaken by events were ignored as he ended his outburst by threatening: "I will get you for this". Subsequently I attempted, each time I met him, to heal the wounds but he was not approachable and he declined a couple of placatory lunch invitations. With good cause I never forgot his 'I-will-get-you-for-this' threat, especially when he became Editor-in-Chief of the Birmingham *Evening Mail* and *Birmingham Post.*

Later on, in times of political unrest at Villa Park, the anti-Doug Ellis publicity in his papers was such that I could easily have concluded that I was the centre of a vendetta. Maybe when I was unseated at Villa Park for three years David Hopkinson was satisfied that he had 'got me'... and all down to my eagerness to keep a promise. Subsequently he left the Birmingham newspapers and later took a senior post with *The Times* in London.

As a result of the Rioch signing hopes were high in August 1969 when Tommy started his first full season as manager, though it proved to be an illusion. By mid-September we had lost seven and drawn two of our first nine games and we were back in an even more serious relegation fight than before.

It was about this time that Tommy told his famous story about my having told him I was "right behind him". "If it's OK by you chairman I'll have you in front of me," was his version. "Then I can see what you're up to..." A joke's a joke, but Tommy wasn't daft. He knew the score. By the end of the year we had played twenty-five Second Division games and had won only four. Gates were not bad, still averaging more than 20,000, but fans were getting alarmed and some of them were now calling him Doctor Dolittle.

He had to go. My first managerial sacking had arrived, and Tommy Docherty accepted it and a relatively handsome cheque, with good grace. Some years later I was interested to note in one of his books, *Docherty*, written by Brian Clarke (Kingswood Press) that Tommy said of me: 'Ellis was a good man in many ways. He had a good side to him.' No doubt he recalled that when the moment came I wasn't behind him, I was facing him and looking him in the eye having honoured, to his satisfaction, the unexpired part of his three-year contract.

To my knowledge he has never since uttered a seriously bad word against either Aston Villa or myself. Indeed there remained a welcome for him at both Villa Park and my home, as he well knew.

The managerial upheaval was not the only factor, in those early years, to attract the sort of headlines that conflicted with a desire for stability and progress. Boardroom unrest, with constant disagreements and changes of directors, continued to undermine our efforts.

Harry Parkes was prone to make what I felt were unhelpful comments in public before he eventually lost his board place, and there were other examples of directors pulling apart rather than working together.

In a three year period between March 1969 and September 1972, the structure of the board changed again and again. Jim Hartley, head of Harmo Industries, was co-opted in March 1969 to be joined later by his friend, Dick Greenhalgh. In May 1971 Greenhalgh and Harry Kartz resigned over differences of opinion and more problems were ahead.

The most acrimonious example was to come in the autumn of 1972 when, in an internal power struggle, I was unseated from the chairmanship and briefly replaced by Jim Hartley.

A month later, after calling an EGM to outline what had gone on, I was given a clear vote of confidence from shareholders and there emerged under my chairmanship a reconstructed board.

Jim Hartley, Harry Parkes and Bob Mackay departed and the new board included Harry Kartz, Eric Houghton, the club's famous former England player and 1957 FA Cup-winning manager, along with Alan Smith, then Warwickshire CCC's captain and England wicketkeeper batsman. For a while the atmosphere was better and in April 1973 I invited Sir William Dugdale, a Villa Park regular, and Harry Cressman of Bristol Street Motors to join the board

In the meantime, however, in January 1970, we were looking for a manager to replace the Doc.

Chapter Six

Cloughie's Bid For Villa Job

A whole variety of incidents have combined to form what I regard as an eventful life in football. One of these started off as a simple car drive to Manchester, but turned out to be a most significant few hours in the history of the club.

When Tommy Docherty was dismissed, after a 5-3 home defeat by Portsmouth on January 17th, 1970, we clearly needed an urgent replacement. Relegation to the Third Division loomed and a virtual clear-out of the coaching staff had left the reserve team coach, Vic Crowe, former captain of Aston Villa and Wales, as the only experienced member of the backroom staff. Vic thus became caretaker manager while the board and myself undertook our first, slightly precarious, search for a new permanent appointment.

To be realistic we did not have too much to offer any established, big-name boss at that time. Just think about it: we were right at the bottom of the Second Division with only seventeen points from twenty-six games, there was little cash available for further new players and the previous manager had lasted little more than a year.

Ominously, that initial lift-off in December 1968 was in danger of leading only to a further crisis and the unpalatable truth was that Aston Villa was in the second worst plight of its entire ninety-six years. Though an immediate appointment was needed there had never been any intention of offering it to Vic Crowe who, in personality and image was the exact opposite to the Doc.

I was sifting through what I now know is the usual crop of applications from a few 'possibles', a host of no-hopers and the odd crank when I travelled to Manchester with Vic to watch a player.

During what proved to be an enlightening drive I got to talk to him seriously, at length, perhaps for the first time and as we chatted that scouting trip became a successful job interview.

Long before we arrived back I realised that this Welsh-born true Brummie was Aston Villa to the core, a very serious-minded professional and a man with an absolute desire to see Aston Villa on top of the football world. That was precisely what I wanted, too. Why look any further? Vic attended the next Board meeting expecting, at best, to be asked to remain as caretaker manager for the rest of the season but walked out as a permanent appointment.

History now reminds us that it was too late to avoid relegation to the Third Division, but it also reminds us that he was ultimately to complete the U-turn from disaster that Tommy Docherty had inherited and had moved in the right direction.

As I said earlier, two more contrasting characters it would be difficult to imagine. Where Doc was volatile, controversial, the master of the quick quote, not too bothered about whom he upset, Vic thought before he spoke, thought twice before he acted, weighed everything up carefully, and left others to make the shock-horror headlines.

In his first full season, now with former playing colleague Ron Wylie back as his assistant manager, we finished fourth in the Third Division and took a huge following with us on the rounds of the tiny, dilapidated little grounds where our visit was like a cup-tie.

But Vic truly made his mark as a manager by reaching the Football League Cup Final after a magnificent pre-Christmas, semi-final victory over Manchester United that middle-aged and older fans still recall with relish. Later, at Wembley, even the London-based press confirmed that we played better football than our distinguished First Division opponents, Spurs, who won with a couple of goals by Martin Chivers after being forced to chase us for much of the match.

We set new attendance records around the Third Division, while of the 100,000 gate at Wembley, 30,000 were Villa fans.

During his four years as manager Vic Crowe bought selectively and shrewdly with such performers as Andy Lochhead, Jim Cumbes, Ray Graydon, Chris Nicholl, Ian Ross, John Gidman, Sammy Morgan and John

Robson completely raising the standard of the team. A young player named Brian Little had begun to make his mark, with other juniors also progressing well. We had purchased our training ground at Bodymoor Heath and the club as a whole was moving forward.

The Third Division Championship in 1971-72 was followed by a tantalising third place in Division Two and no-one was sorrier than I when a disappointing final few weeks of 1973-74 saw us slip back to 14th in Division Two.

Vic Crowe, I know for certain, found it unsettling as manager to be aware that there was little unanimity at board level.

All of this was a great pity since we had made a trading profit of £35,000 in our first year, quite a turn-around from the £200,000-worth of debts and mounting losses we had inherited.

Even when we went into the Third Division we took a record £50,000 in advance sales and, by the end of that Wembley season, we made a trading profit of £84,452, quite a handsome figure at that time.

Off-the-field activities were getting better, too, with *Aston Villa News & Record,* our match-day programme, winning awards and all-round facilities being gradually up-graded.

Soon after the 1968 change-over the long-serving secretary, Fred Archer, had retired, to be replaced by Alan Bennett, who had been assistant secretary at Chelsea, and his more modern thinking also helped to improve our administration, plus my continual insistence in the philosophy of giving our supporters a much more personal service as valued customers and listening to their views.

Extensive efforts were being made on the commercial side to meet my aim, publicly expressed when I took the chairmanship, to capitalise in every possible club-related way.

In this regard, with Eric Woodward in charge of the commercial side, we were a pioneering outfit, using many of the principles we had both witnessed in American sport.

In this country advertising tended to be very restrained at that time, whereas the Americans would cleverly use television as an instant, visual means of catching the consumer's eye.

In the world of the 1990s we have caught up with them to a large extent but two decades ago we were distinctly feeling our way at Villa Park.

I well remember an amusing episode which demonstrates the efforts we made to establish more firmly the advantages of advertisers using football and television as an ideal combined medium to display their wares and their company name.

Harry Cressman, chairman of Bristol Street Motors, was persuaded that he should have a pitch-side advertising board at the ground on the theory that, apart from being there on show before the live, captive audience at each home match, it would also get some national screen coverage when our games were televised. We asked him for a sum of £3,000 for the board on the 'TV side' of the stadium opposite the set camera position. In reply he wanted to know how much TV time he could expect his advertisement to receive and we forecast about three minutes, i.e. £1,000 per minute, plus twenty-odd home games when it would be seen by thousands for a couple of hours or so as an added attraction.

Harry wasn't convinced. So we did a deal with him. He would have the board with no down-payment, but he would owe us £3,000 if he got his three minutes on TV, a situation that would have to be carefully monitored. As the season in question was approaching its conclusion the board had been on screen for a total of some two minutes. Danger signs were flashing. Unless we helped the situation along a little we would miss out on that three thousand pounds.

A big home fixture was coming up with TV coverage planned so we let it be known to the players that it would be in all our interests if that particular advertisement were in camera shot as long as possible.

Sure enough, in the nick of time, our winger Willie Anderson went down heavily under a challenge and his 'injury' was such that the physio had to run on to give him attention as the camera kept rolling.

To our delight the episode went out on screen as the BSM board proclaimed the merits of Ford motor cars. By the final fixture, when a full count was carried out the advertising board had received in excess of three minutes exposure and a satisfied Harry Cressman sent us his cheque for £3,000.

Willie Anderson 'survived' his 'injury', and some quarter of a century on, this form of advertising brings the club a very substantial annual income.

However, I was always totally committed to the intention that Aston Villa would constantly move forward and not slip back. So, in the summer of 1974, we sadly, and with genuine appreciation of what they had done, dispensed with the services of Vic Crowe and Ron Wylie. Another phase of the campaign lay ahead. Another new manager was required.

At that time any top club had merely to say "we need a new manager" and the public would clamour, with ample justification, for Brian Clough.

This was especially the case with Aston Villa, though our supporters have never previously realised how near he was to becoming our manager, nor how keenly he told me he wanted the job. My first indication came in December 1972 when Vic Crowe successfully negotiated with Clough to sign England Under-21 full-back, John Robson, for £90,000 from Derby County.

The deal had been settled at the Baseball Ground, Vic had gone off with the player to his home and I found myself alone in the small Baseball Ground boardroom with Clough and his assistant, Peter Taylor.

Since then it has been written in Clough's autobiography by John Sadler, of how the pair had a 'wearing down' technique when they wanted to get their own way by standing one each side of their subject and talking to that person in turn to the total confusion of the victim. This was precisely the situation in which I quite unexpectedly found myself. At first I wondered if I could believe the evidence of my own ears.

The Clough-Taylor partnership was then the most effective in club football with five years of headline-making progress behind them. Also, as it was to transpire, the First Division Championship was on its way to the Baseball Ground the following May.

To the best of everyone's knowledge, outside of those closest to the club, their fiery relationship with the then chairman Sam Longson would go on and on as long as Derby County were successful.

How wrong we all were. "Shut the door..." said one. "Shall I tell him or you?" replied the other. "No, you tell him," came the quick-fire, seemingly well-rehearsed rejoinder.

"Look, Mr Ellis... fetch us." By now I was feeling totally bemused. My only purpose in being there, remember, was to successfully support my manager in purchasing one of County's players.

"Fetch us?" I replied. "What do you mean?" "Fetch us... to Villa," added one of them.

"That's right, Mr Ellis. Fetch us to Villa..." confirmed the other.

"We'll come and make you the most successful chairman in the country. We'll win some trophies for you," went on the double act.

My first reaction was to be stunned speechless. My second was to protest. Our manager, Vic Crowe, was serving us well and had only just walked out the very door which they had just closed behind him.

I know I was subsequently to get the label 'Deadly' pinned on me but no way would I have treated Vic or anyone else in such a 'deadly' fashion.

It's true that Vic was subsequently dismissed, but by then I felt he had been given a fair crack of the whip.

"Come off it, chaps," I said. "You know very well we've already got a manager who is serving us well." Cloughie's reply sticks in my mind to this very day. "Oh, f--k him," he said. "He'll never win you anything. You'll do no good with him." Needless to say I cut the conversation short, but it was not the only time Brian Clough made a strong play to become manager of Aston Villa FC.

There was the time when he contacted me through an intermediary to say that he was available to become manager of Aston Villa but could not officially apply. I sent a message back saying that, on this occasion, I was in a position to interview him but his application had to be in writing before we could approach his club to formally request permission.

The intermediary came back to me and said that although Brian would not apply in writing he wished to meet me for a chat and to verbally offer his services. His suggestion was that we met at a restaurant in Derby.

Fat chance of that, I thought. It will be straight into the local papers the moment we are recognised.

In the event I chose somewhere a shade more discreet, namely the Corn Exchange restaurant in Lichfield, owned by a salmon fishing friend of mine, Maurice Nock, where we could be a little less obvious. How naive I must have been. From the moment we arrived Brian put himself right on show, chatting to anyone who approached him, signing autographs, the lot. Discreet, my eye! Possibly he wanted someone to ring the newspapers to get the rumour going nicely and sound the alarm bells at his club. I was never quite sure, but I had my suspicions. Maybe he wanted me to offer him the job so that he could put pressure on his own club before turning it down.

Again, I was never sure.

With so much uncertainty in my mind the outcome of our meal and chat was me telling him: "Look, Brian. It would never work. There is only one boss at Aston Villa and that's me.

"You and I could never work together." After the meal I drove him in my Rolls to my farm in Lichfield where we sat in the car with rain cascading down outside, as he attempted to persuade me to change my mind.

He didn't succeed but, give him his due, he apparently never gave up trying, though I continued to wonder whether he wanted a Villa approach to use as a lever at his own club. He left Derby County, remember, in a storm of controversy in 1973.

On a third occasion a writer named Jim Waters, now deceased, of the *Evening Mail* and *Sports Argus,* Birmingham, went to interview Cloughie at Majorca where he had gone on one of his famous breaks.

The journalist, who lived at Derby and was a County fanatic, had correctly heard that all was not well between manager and club and felt that, if he turned up unexpectedly at the poolside for a general chat the story would come out.

How right he was. As the pool-side socialising flowed so Cloughie opened up about how he would gladly leave Derby and join Aston Villa, a sentiment expressed in his own colourful and inimitable fashion.

It was even better than Jim Waters had expected. The next day the *Mail* was able to carry a banner headline exclusive quoting Clough as saying: "Come on Doug, I'm ready to crawl on broken glass to Aston Villa... if you've got the guts to come and get me," or words to that effect.

The story was packed with the usual, forceful Clough observations, all aired in public, questioning my resolve, and putting me in an impossible position. It killed off any hopes there might have been of forging a sensible Chairman-Manager relationship which I continue to insist is absolutely essential for long-term, if not short-term, club success.

I still didn't think it would work and I've never changed my mind. There will be those who will believe I was wrong and that I should have let him have his head. All I can suggest is that Nottingham Forest, for all their trophies during the best years of Brian Clough, have also had more than their fair share of problems including a temporary loss of financial stability, a spell out of the FA Premiership and a change in ownership.

Chapter Seven

Downside Of Saunders

The selection of Ron Saunders to succeed Vic Crowe as manager in the summer of 1974 was not a universally popular move with either public or press, though he was to prove the most successful of the club's first century.

Because of his reputation as a stern-faced, sergeant-major type who was extremely selective with whom he co-operated, not everyone warmed to him. This 'image' thing apart, however, he had steered Norwich City to the Second Division Championship in 1972 and to the League Cup Final a year later before moving to Manchester City.

At Maine Road he reached another League Cup Final in his first five months but, after losing to Wolves at Wembley he was dismissed.

It was not, of course, the League Cup Final defeat that cost him his job but his uneasy relationship with big-name, star players who could not easily accept his military-style methods. 'Player Power' as it was described at the time.

Such well-established internationals as Mike Summerbee, Peter Barnes, Colin Bell, Joe Royle and the like were at the club at that time and there were reports of serious dressing room disagreements with the new manager.

Consequently, when Aston Villa were looking for a successor to Vic Crowe, one with the experience to get the best out of the excellent squad of players left behind, Ron Saunders was readily available. He was recommended by Alf Ramsey, whom we had interviewed, but who had made it clear he would not move his home from Ipswich and this was a non-starter.

Let me say here that it has always been my way to ensure that new members of staff with specific duties are made aware from the start exactly where they stand with regard to responsibility and authority.

That principle set the tone of my ensuing relationship with Ron Saunders in the first few weeks of his reign as a manager.

One night, around 10pm, during his first pre-season he called me at home from the Penns Hall Hotel where he was staying, to say that he had signed Frank Carrodus from his former club, Manchester City, for £100,000. I had never even heard of the player's name, that's how little consultation there had been.

"Oh no you haven't," I replied. "You don't have the authority to commit the club to that amount of money." "Sorry, chairman," he replied. "The deal has been completed." "Stay where you are," I said. "I'm coming over..." Penns Hall is only about ten minutes drive from my home so I was in his twin-bedded hotel room in a flash. I sat on one bed. He sat on the other.

Ron protested that it was too late to stop the deal so I insisted on telephoning Peter Swales, the Manchester City chairman, who was himself in bed by now. My call didn't please Ron, but it had to be made.

Swales insisted that our manager had shaken hands on the deal which was thus sealed and still on, to which I replied: "No way..." Crack of dawn next day Peter called me and said one of his directors was journeying to Villa Park to discuss the matter with me.

In the meantime Ron had explained to me that Carrodus would be a big asset to our team inasmuch as while not the classiest of players he would run all day. He was a great workhorse, the sort of player every team needs, Ron explained, in the sort of consultation that ought to have taken place before not after the deal was set up.

Subsequently, of course, we have had similar types in Des Bremner, from the Championship-European Cup-winning team and, currently under John Gregory, Ian Taylor.

I was never in dispute with Ron Saunders about the team-building logic of signing Carrodus, merely his absence of consultation and lack of courtesy.

When the Manchester City director, Dr Rose, arrived next day, I sat down with him, reduced the fee from £100,000 to £90,000, a useful ten per cent saving and Frank Carrodus joined Aston Villa, the right way, to give us excellent service. However, getting off on the wrong foot in that way possibly soured the relationship between Ron Saunders and myself thereafter.

Ron then signed Welsh international Leighton Phillips, from Cardiff, soon after the start of the season and, following an indifferent run to Christmas, got the team's act together in outstanding fashion.

Our promotion aim was achieved, as runners-up behind Manchester United, and the League Cup was won, against Saunders' former club Norwich at Wembley. At the end of the season Ron Saunders was selected as Bell's Whisky Manager of the Year, ahead of Dave Mackay who had succeeded Brian Clough at Derby County and had won the First Division Championship.

It completed a remarkable first season with the club for Saunders, and all the better possibly for his getting his demarcation lines understood. Yet he had a rather strange sense of humour. By chance the final match of his first season, when promotion was assured, was at Norwich whom he had left amid forceful criticism he made of the then chairman, the eminent Sir Arthur South JP.

When we started the return journey home, we arrived at a roundabout adjacent to Sir Arthur's business premises, a furrier's shop.

Ron instructed the coach driver to go around that roundabout two or three times while all our players were asked to give the two-finger sign to Sir Arthur's place. He seemed to derive a good deal of amusement and satisfaction from the rather childish display.

However, any critical recollections I have of Saunders are well-balanced by my admiration for him as a strict-disciplinarian who made many excellent buys, built possibly three successful Villa teams and had the knack of getting the best out of his players. Never would I belittle or undermine these achievements in any way because while Ron Saunders was manager, the club achieved the targets set at the time of the 1968 upheaval.

His team went on to win the Championship and the European Cup, the latter after he had resigned, and there are no higher club accolades than that and no better confirmation of his managerial prowess.

In his second season he bought Dennis Mortimer and Andy Gray, excellent purchases both of them as indeed were the majority of his signings.

On the other hand it is fair to say that he was a most difficult person to deal with, a manager who was never comfortable with any high-profile players who attracted publicity. He gave me the impression of being jealous of any who did.

During those years, when the public were acutely aware of the tensions that existed between Ron Saunders and myself, individual players were also having an extremely rough ride with their manager, notably one particular club servant who simply did not deserve to be treated as he was.

I refer to Charles Aitken. The full extent of Charlie's experiences were only brought home to me in full detail later when he became a much-respected club vice-president for a three year period during my second spell as chairman.

It was in 1976 that Charlie's distinguished 16-year playing career was terminated in what, to this day, I regard as an utterly disgraceful and unfeeling fashion by Ron Saunders.

Just to put the matter into fair perspective let us recall that Charlie had joined Villa as a boy from Edinburgh junior football in 1959, had made his debut as a teenager, played non-stop first-team football until he was 34 and in so doing had set up a club record of 656 full appearances.

During that time he had caused not so much as a ripple of dissent in the club as he went about his business with all the dedication of the ultimate in model professionals. Understandably, against such a background, the sense of injustice had lingered on in Charlie's memory when he later described to me how his distinguished Aston Villa career came to an end in what he called 'total degradation'.

One day in December 1975, while still in the first team, he was called into the manager's office and told that he could stay at Villa Park as long as he liked and whatever he did in the future would be his own decision. Charlie thanked him but, wanting to play on as long as possible, volunteered no observations about future retirement.

Yet, some three weeks after that meeting he played his last game for the club, against QPR in January 1976. Without giving a reason the manager stopped picking him for any of his teams, though he remained one of the fittest players at the club, forced him to train on his own, banned him from the first-team dressing room and only spoke to him just once more.

This is Charlie Aitken's own description of how he was discarded, and I have no cause to disbelieve him. A few minutes before the March transfer deadline for moves he was called in and told that he had been released on a 'free'. At some stage he could have a testimonial match. No further discussion. Goodbye.

This, I am assured, is how the club's longest-serving player was summarily discharged.

Fortunately he was snapped up by New York Cosmos, Pele and all, and in that way his playing career did end on a high note, no thanks to Aston Villa. His sense of grievance was such that it was many years before he could bring himself to return to Villa Park. When he did bury the hatchet and make friends with the club again he was welcomed back with open arms and virtually given the run of the place. That is how highly we regarded him on his return.

Charles has many stories to tell about Saunders, whose training methods, team coaching and trophy-winning achievements he still holds in the very highest esteem. 'One-hundred per cent efficient' is how he has described his training routines and match preparation schedules. Indeed, he found him 'friendly, chatty and agreeable' in his first season despite the stories he had heard from his mate, Mike Summerbee, at Maine Road. Then he appeared to undergo a complete change of attitude when he had brought some success to the club.

Why, then, the contradiction between the man's unquestioned qualities and what appeared to be ruthless disregard of his victims' finer feelings? Aitken's theory is that Ron suffered from an inferiority complex and it was this that constantly spurred him to prove to anyone with a public profile that he held the upper hand.

He certainly left Aitken, an Aston Villa man to his core, with some remarkable memories. One story he tells is of an occasion when some of the players went to the PFA's televised annual dinner where Jasper Carrott was speaking.

In his own inimitable fashion Jasper poked fun at just about everyone, including Ron Saunders. One comment he made caused widespread laughter and the camera panned onto the face of Jim Cumbes throwing his head back and having a good hearty laugh, just as he would have done had the wisecrack been about anyone, most of all himself, knowing Jim and his sense of humour.

It was all part of the lighter side of the game yet, apparently, at the next training session Saunders accused Cumbes of being in league with Jasper to cause him public ridicule. Jim is the mildest of men but he was annoyed at the ludicrous accusation, answered back sharply and, it seems, there was an unseemly training ground 'incident' involving the two of them. Such friction was, by all accounts, a regular feature.

No-one suffered more from the indignities he could impose than his coach Roy McLaren. One day the manager asked for opinions on a particular point, Roy seemingly offered one, and was instantly pounced on, verbally, by his boss. Saunders humiliated him in front of the players for being "completely wrong" and then added: "Right. You are now a goal post". There followed a practice match on an impromptu area and Roy McLaren, who later went to live in Australia, was instructed to stand for a considerable time doing the job of one of the goalposts. It was said to be a joke, but no-one noticed Roy McLaren laughing.

Charles Aitken, like myself, believes that Ron Saunders would have remained at Villa Park as the club's greatest manager, which his outstanding record endorses, but for the inexplicable other side of his nature. Also Ron Saunders was a manager who would involve himself in what might be termed 'club politics', running with the hare and hunting with hounds, I called it. I knew for a fact that he would visit the homes of other directors for discussions aimed at undermining my position as Chairman, a distinct policy of 'divide and conquer'.

He was always money-orientated, greedy even, demanding double bonuses to any of those received by the players and not liking his backroom staff to be rewarded in similar fashion.

I vividly remember one occasion, during the time when I had handed over the chairmanship to Sir William Dugdale, due largely to the manager's involvement in board affairs and was serving just as a director, I recommended at a board meeting in the manager's presence that a £250 bonus should be paid to our youth coach Frank Upton and our chief scout Neville Briggs, in recognition of the achievements of the youth scheme.

The silence that greeted my proposal was deafening. To my amazement Ron Saunders would not support the suggestion and because of this the chairman turned it down. In all my years in business and football I had never heard a head of department turn down a bonus that had been recommended by his directors for his or her staff who deserved it.

Later I was told that Ron had observed privately that if there were any bonuses to be had they should go to him.

Ron Saunders had huge qualities as a leader of footballers and a builder of football teams but in my opinion he did not like anyone who had a high profile whom he thought might get more public attention than he did.

Because of the big turn around in the club's situation since 1968 I tended to get a lot of publicity myself, and this he clearly did not like any more than he liked individual players being in the headlines.

It led to a lot of tensions between us and more than one intense disagreement.

The question of Saunders and his problems with the star names at Maine Road often sprang to my mind in his dealings at Villa Park.

To me such players as John Gidman, Andy Gray, John Gregory, Chris Nicholl and others, were all sold too soon, even if it is true that trophies were subsequently won without them. All these were players with strong views of their own.

There was the occasion in 1977, during Sir William's chairmanship, when Andy Gray was chosen by his peers for the Professional Footballers' Association's Player and Young Player Awards. Andy, rightly proud of the dual selection by playing colleagues, was required to attend the PFA's annual presentation dinner in London to collect his trophies. All he required was the formality of club approval.

The dinner was on a Sunday night, players from virtually every club in the League were in attendance having chosen playing colleagues whom they admired and respected for annual awards. The concept had originally been put together by Eric Woodward, Villa's commercial manager who, after all, was present and would have looked after Andy, if necessary.

But Ron Saunders said "no, you can't go", because of the League Cup Final replay against Everton at Hillsborough the following Wednesday.

The PFA then offered a chauffeur-driven car each way, with a promise that Andy would be home in bed, stone-cold sober, before midnight. Ron Saunders still said no. I firmly believe that Andy was too popular for him. Journalists have told me that if, at an after-the-match press conference he was asked something like "what did you think of Andy Gray's two goals" he would reply "Frank Carrodus was our best player..."

PFA officials were distraught at their function being devalued in this way so, as a weak compromise, the trophy presentation was made by Chris Nicholl in Andy's garden, filmed in advance, and screened at the dinner.

I sometimes wonder if Andy ever forgave him. I have been told since that he accepted his manager's decision like the good pro he was, but realised afterwards that he had been denied what would have been an important hour or two in his life. Incidentally, I was thrilled when he won his well-deserved Commentator of the Year award in recognition of his effervescent work for Sky TV.

This disregard by Ron Saunders of players enjoying their moments of glory contrasted sharply with the situation when Ron was named as Bell's Manager of the Year while we were on an end-of-season Caribbean Tour in 1975 after our promotion-League Cup success.

On this occasion our manager was adamant about being flown back home, first-class, with his wife who was on the trip, to receive his award and a cheque for £1,000 from Eric Morecambe at the Café Royal and then flown back to the Caribbean. Talk about dual standards! The manager can fly back and forth across the Atlantic for HIS award. In contrast a star player was not allowed a chauffeur-driven return trip from Birmingham to London.

Strangely, although he had by now crossed the Atlantic three times, Ron's fear of flying caused us problems on that trip. We had just one match to play, in Barbados, in order to establish that this was a working trip, not a mere holiday.

We had a week in St Lucia, a week of absolute luxury on the Cunard Princess cruising around the West Indies en route for Bridgetown, Barbados, until a fire in the engine room left us adrift without power for twenty-six hours. Eventually we docked in the Dutch East Indies, some 800 miles from our destination and without the necessary liner to complete the journey.

I hired two small thirty or thirty-six seater aircraft to ferry our party, which included wives, to Bridgetown. Our manager and a director and a leading player were so nervous at the prospect that they wanted us to charter a KLM jet that was available to fly us to Amsterdam and return home without playing the fixture.

This we couldn't do since we were committed and eventually, under protest, Ron was persuaded to fly with the rest of us and the fixture was played. It was just as well that we made it, just in time, because when the news got through to Barbados that the fixture was in danger there was a threat of serious unrest among disappointed supporters.

There were riot police in and around the ground.

In the event we received a terrific welcome. The Ambassador was waiting with tears in his eyes and said: "Thanks, fellows. Thank God, you came. You have no idea what the radio and newspapers have been saying about the English."

We won by about seven or eight goals and subsequently I received a letter of thanks from the Foreign Office for the efforts we had made.

Twenty-six hours adrift at sea with no engines, no electricity and no air conditioning sorted out the men from the boys. And the babies. I'm not saying who was which, but I did vow we would NOT take wives and girlfriends on club trips, a rule which I have subsequently relaxed.

To be fair, out-of-season club tours over the years have been a rich source of amusing episodes as one would expect in a holiday atmosphere when normal pressures have been temporarily left behind.

A couple of what were, to me anyway, hilarious examples of this came in the early days when we were in Dar-Es-Salaam to play the Tanzanian national team.

During our visit we were taken into the game park on safari to watch at close quarters a whole variety of exotic beasts running wild.

Our party was split into three or four suitably armoured vehicles, each with a port-hole large enough for a couple of people at a time to poke their heads out and either watch, perhaps through field glasses, or if the animals were close enough, take still or moving pictures of lions, giraffes or whatever.

Our front truck contained half-a-dozen or so members of the playing staff and, players being players, there were three heads, instead of the maximum of two for which the aperture was safely designed, jammed in tight. Jimmy Cumbes, our goalkeeper-cricketer, was one. Charlie Aitken, who set a record number of appearances for the club, was another.

Suddenly a rhinoceros, possibly disturbed by the intrusion, decided to make a charge. In a flash, from all being serene one moment, a couple of tons of angry rhino was then hurtling at breakneck speed at the players' vehicle. One of the funniest things I have ever seen in my life was those three heads, with wide, panic-stricken-eyes, all trying to pull out of the hole at the same time and being stuck there because the space was not really big enough for them. They made it. Just about. And the runaway rhino pulled up short. But the trio kept their heads well down after that.

The match itself also leaves an indelible memory of another player who thought his day of reckoning had arrived early.

The little national stadium held only about 25,000 people, but what seemed about 50,000 turned up. Some of them, we were told, had walked about a hundred miles just to watch a well-known English team in action.

There were riot police everywhere and thousands of disappointed

Tanzanians were locked outside when the match kicked off. Unknown to myself and my wife Heidi, sitting in the President's Box with the country's dignitaries, large numbers were trying to climb into the ground.

To stop what might have become disastrous over-crowding the police shot off tear-gas shells with a series of bangs that sounded like gunshots.

To add to the pandemonium the tear-gas was caught by the breeze and wafted into the stand and across the pitch. The Tanzanian players had clearly experienced it all before and they simply fell flat onto their bellies to allow the gas to pass over them. To the inexperienced onlooker, however, it might have seemed that they had been shot.

At the time I happened to be watching Neil Rioch, Bruce's brother on the far side of the pitch.

Poor young Neil thought a war had broken out and that he was in the firing line. He set off for the safety of the tunnel and the dressing rooms like a startled rabbit and a group of people at the entrance to the tunnel scattered to let him through.

I'm sure he never ran as fast before or after those few moments as he feared for his life. In my mind's eye, to this day, I can see his knees pumping up almost to his chin in his haste to reach cover.

No doubt just as I could see the funny side of his plight he would have laughed like a drain had he been able to see his chairman crying like a baby as the tear gas arrived.

As Heidi and I were Guests of Honour, nobody else in the President's Box moved for a while, out of a sort of reluctant politeness. Then, when Heidi reached down to pick up her handbag in search of a handkerchief they took this as a sign that we were leaving.

Quick as a flash the President, the Prime Minister and all the other ministers fled off down the aisle, leaving the two of us crying, coughing and spluttering on our own. Anyone who has inhaled tear-gas will understand how unpleasant an experience it was. Eventually I got Heidi to the dressing room, along with the players, to help splash water on her eyes and face and relieve some of the discomfort. Not many matches have actually moved me to tears. This one certainly did...

However, Ron Saunders' determined style of management won us the Football League Cup for a second time when we beat Everton at the third attempt at Old Trafford after draws at Wembley and Hillsborough. By now he had added more excellent signings to the team in Alex Cropley from Arsenal and John Burridge from Blackpool, while Gordon Cowans and

John Deehan had been schooled through the junior system to follow Brian Little's lead.

All of which reminds me of my smart, expensive Italian suit... Through my business travels I had come across a wonderful tailor in San Remo, Italy, from whom I had ordered this superb suit of the finest mohair cloth with an eye-catching sheen on it.

That particular period when Ron's team was earning a fourth place in the First Division while also reaching the Football League Cup Final, with three semi-final games against QPR and a Final and two replays, with extra time, against Everton, were just about as emotional as you could get.

Once the final whistle sounded at Old Trafford, and we had won 3-2 after extra time, having drawn the first replay at Hillsborough, we were all on a tremendous high.

Normally I would not go into the dressing room until the manager and players had enjoyed say fifteen minutes of privacy and bear in mind I was not chairman at this time. On this occasion I was so exhilarated that I made the mistake of rushing straight in as the bubbly corks were popping and players were doing everything but turn somersaults.

As I appeared through the dressing room door, about four pairs of arms reached out – I seem to recall they belonged to Chris Nicholl, Ray Graydon, Chico Hamilton and Ian Ross, though memory is a shade hazy – and into the bath I went. Head first. And wearing my shiny, expensive, San Remo, hand-tailored suit.

For a while, however, that was the last thing on my mind. As I splashed into the bath my head went backwards, under water, and in the boisterous horse-play, it was being held there as water went into my mouth and up my nose and simultaneously Ray Graydon was tipping champagne all over me. It was a prank that nearly went badly wrong. I was half-drowning and very relieved when I eventually got out and I was supplied with a track suit to travel home in on the coach while the soggy, crumpled Italian job went into the skip with muddy shirts, shorts and socks.

One bizarre follow-up to my unscheduled, fully-clothed bath sticks in my mind. As I came out of the dressing room dripping wet I met one of the other directors, the American Harry Cressman, one of the brothers who founded Bristol Street Motors Group.

He realised what had happened and, to my astonishment, he went into the dressing room and jumped into the bath, fully clothed, emerging later to also travel home in a track suit.

DEADLY!

All the way down the M6 we were surrounded by a cavalcade of about a thousand motor cars escorting us all the way with horns sounding and their passengers waving scarves and the like.

On the surface all was well. Underneath? Turmoil.

It was all rather unfortunate, bearing in mind how well things were progressing at the club, that unrest at Board level persisted and was to lead to my leaving Villa Park for three years, other than watching as a fan, having earlier relinquished the chairmanship.

Chapter Eight

Outflanked By Bendall

The most difficult task I have found in attempting to relive periods of club history from two and three decades ago is to put the boardroom unrest of the 1970s into fair perspective without being either too long, totally boring, or both.

Readers will not wish to rake over all the details of share transactions, requisition notices for extraordinary general meetings and circular letters to shareholders from one faction or the other.

It is the outcome of the boardoom politics rather than the fine detail of it that is of importance.

One big help has been the fact that, since I began these up-to-date memoirs I have unearthed among some old papers an actual account of it all which I wrote during the 1979-82 period when I was in exile.

The manuscript is far too long and detailed to reproduce fully here, but I do believe that from it a picture emerges of an individual whose fairly brief involvement in Villa affairs played a significant role in those turbulent days of the 1970s.

During the season 1974-75 when Ron Saunders' team was winning promotion from the Second Division I was invited by the late Trevor Gill, the chairman of the old Villa Vice-Presidents' Lounge, to have lunch with an associate and himself. The third person concerned was a man of considerable means, already a club shareholder, who wished to invest more capital into the club. Trevor Gill was, among other things, an auctioneer, an immaculately-dressed gentleman in a traditional sort of way, a person of precise manners and presentation, he specialised in the auction of goods from business liquidations, an activity that brought him into close contact with our lunch companion.

The three of us duly dined at the Plough and Harrow in Hagley Road, not far from the Birmingham city centre. Trevor Gill's associate was the late Ron Bendall. None of us can rewrite history to our own design. Were it possible I would remove that lunch date from my bygone diary. Little did I know it then, but Mr Bendall was probably already plotting to successfully have me removed first from the chairmanship and then from the board of directors. Ron Bendall was, to put it mildly an unusual man. Exceedingly tall, broad and bulky, slightly stooping, not a handsome individual, he had bushy, prominent eyebrows above facial expressions one could not always fathom.

He was an accountant, the head of a firm specialising in receiverships, and a very successful one at that. Bankruptcies were part of his stock-in-trade, and one would assume that six years earlier Aston Villa FC would have interested him merely for that purpose were it not for the fact that his son, Donald, was a Villa fanatic and season ticket holder. Ronald seemed to have little knowledge of or interest in football, or Aston Villa, other than the going rate of shares.

I had no reason to believe that Bendall senior had any hidden agenda at that time especially since, ironically, he had signed an EGM requisition notice a couple of years earlier to support me in the removal from the board of three warring directors.

During the meal it transpired that he wished to purchase more shares to add to those already held by his family and himself, and to become a director. I responded by informing him of the restriction that no director should own more than five per cent of the company. This was to ensure that we all honoured an undertaking I had made to this effect at a gathering of 3,000 shareholders and potential shareholders at the flotation meeting at Villa Park on April 5th, 1969.

However, under the club constitution a vacancy existed on the board, so against this background and after our Plough and Harrow discussions, Ron Bendall was invited to join us on condition that his and his family's shareholding was a maximum of 5,000 at £5 each. With a maximum of seven directors this would total a combined holding of not more than thirty-five per cent, the remaining sixty-five per cent being available to the public at large, should they choose to take it up.

In the interim period, to help the finances of the club, I had made an interest-free loan of £100,000, taking up as security an option to convert the loan into 20,000 shares at £5 each. The understanding was that I would recover the loan as and when the club was back in the First Division with no debts and a sum of £500,000 in the bank. This situation was subsequently achieved and we were reminded by Harry Cressman that it was now appropriate for me to recover the loan while rescinding the option to take up the 20,000 shares.

The promise was duly honoured, but to the detriment of my own position. Within the next few months at successive board meetings Mr Bendall introduced the transfer of shares under the names of his two sons and himself, totalling 27.2 per cent of the company's equity. Naturally I reminded him of the stipulation he had accepted when he joined the board but, to this, Harry Cressman responded: "Ten years have elapsed since you committed yourself to supporters and shareholders. There is now no need to cap individual holdings."

I was stunned speechless by Harry's remarks because only a short time earlier I had relinquished my option somewhat reluctantly since it was at a distinct disadvantage to me. At that time Harold Wilson's wealth tax left me with only a tiny proportion of my income so I would have much preferred to leave the money invested in the club. However, I went along with the principle to keep faith with the promise I had made to shareholders and supporters, yet here it was being overturned in favour of a newcomer to the board. So much for trust and unity.

It was around this time that another remarkable example of board disunity took place. Our youth set-up was keen on signing a player from Liverpool schools, Frank Pimblett, but it looked as though we would lose out to another club whom we suspected were bending the pay rules on signing such players.

In order to help us to sign him I visited the player's home in Liverpool where I found his family to be on hard times in the kind of stark conditions found there in the mid-seventies.

Pimblett's mother was asking for terms that were simply not permissible, to meet what another club had agreed and this I overcame by promising to meet their requirements when he was eighteen, which would comply with the appropriate regulations.

One problem remained. The lad had no decent gear to wear to join other, better-off young professionals, so I arranged for a couple of new outfits to be purchased for him so that he could arrive at the club with his head held high.

The next thing I knew was that I had been reported to the FA by my own board colleagues for breaking regulations. I saw a copy of the letter sent from Villa Park so I was left in no doubt about who had 'reported' me. Would you believe that... my own board colleagues?

Down I had to go to Lancaster Gate, to answer charges of illegal inducement and I expected to have a fine imposed of about £1,000. When it was time to speak up on my own behalf I explained how I had found the lad, in a very poor home, keen to join Aston Villa but embarrassed at being unable to clothe himself adequately. I received a sympathetic hearing about my trivial offence and a fine of £500 was imposed. This, to the FA's surprise, I paid in full, on the spot, in banknotes having taken with me the sum of £1,000 which I expected we would have to pay, thanks to treachery from within.

In my account of that entire period, written back in 1979 I refer to myself as having been the victim of 'knife-in-the-back tactics and skulduggery' and outline the following scenario. Following the AGM of 1975, a hugely successful one in the wake of the promotion-League Cup double, I returned from holiday in Norway to find that secret meetings had been taking place among other directors. One meeting, I gleaned, had been at the bedside of Ron Bendall when he was in hospital for a spell.

Unknown to myself they had decided that I should be relieved of the chairmanship and replaced by Sir William Dugdale, then Sheriff of the County of Warwickshire, with myself being demoted to a place on the board. My first reaction was one of extreme anger, to tell them to go to hell, but I quickly had second thoughts. The club is always bigger than the individual and badly needed a period of harmony. If I could continue to serve the club as a director while, after seven years at the helm, someone else took the ultimate responsibility, why not? During those seven years, without my daily attention, my own travel business had gone into serious decline, making a £250,000 loss on the last financial year, a significant amount at that time.

Taking everything into account I agreed to take a back seat, serve under Bill Dugdale, head of a family of true Villa folk and still a friend, and hopefully continue to see the club progress from the dark days of pre-1968.

Bill was a good professional chairman of meetings, but he lacked experience of being in charge of a football club. Having been 'born with a silver spoon in his mouth' he was unused to the machinations of a hard-headed pro like Ron Saunders and the more experienced players.

Sometimes other directors and myself were aghast at his lack of know-how in dealing with commercial enterprises and architects and builders carrying out work around the stadium.

Thus changes had been made at the top, but stability had not been achieved. Ron Saunders was being allowed to rule his staff by fear and create a bad atmosphere in the club with what I believed was his manipulation of directors.

In 1978 Ron Bendall approached me and asked if I would support him in putting his son Donald, a friendly and seemingly well-meaning young man, up against Alan Smith who was up for re-election at the next AGM. Bendall senior was a tax exile who spent most of his time in the Isle of Man. It would obviously suit him to have a foot in the boardroom back at Villa Park. I could see the sense of it but declined to give an answer because I was not happy about the situation as a whole.

Whilst I was hesitating it came as a complete surprise to me to hear that Sir William together with Harry Cressman and Alan Smith had called a press conference to announce their resignation from the board a few days before the August AGM. Ron Bendall was putting up Harry Kartz as the next chairman, obviously as his front man, plus son Donald, which left me isolated alongside Eric Houghton, who was now approaching his seventies.

I did not oppose the appointment of Harry as chairman. He was an old friend and racing associate of mine but after the changes had been made I was astonished to find that a new contract had already been agreed for the manager, Ron Saunders. More behind-the-scenes lobbying, no doubt.

They were awarding him a six-year contract with a three-year revolvement, quite unnecessarily I felt since his existing contract still had two years to run. I'm well aware that, here, it will be pointed out that in 1977 the League Cup had been won for the second time and that within that new six-year deal the First Division Championship was on its way.

My response is that well before the six years had been completed Ron Saunders walked out on Aston Villa in the advanced stages of the European Cup-winning campaign. I wasn't with the club at that time but there was enough publicity on the subject for everyone to be aware that by now he wanted his famous (notorious?) 'roll-over' contract.

By this time the Bendall family held some twenty-seven per cent of the club's issued share capital in direct contravention of our earlier principles. To cut a long story short I decided to call an EGM with the objective of getting Ronald and Donald Bendall along with Harry Kartz removed from the board. On the night the voting figures, as compared to the proxies, were interesting. When the formalities were completed it emerged that he had taken his 27.2 per cent to 44 per cent of the votes while I took my five per cent to 42 per cent and lost out narrowly, despite getting a large majority of ordinary shareholders on my side at the actual meeting before it became a ballot.

After that my board place became untenable and eventually I resigned and sold my stake to Ron Bendall with an agreement that should he ever sell it would be to me at par, namely five pounds each.

Subsequently, in 1982, after more wheeling and dealing, he honoured that promise though at considerably more than five pounds each and after craftily getting one over on me, yet again. That's another story. First I had to learn to endure life without Aston Villa as the club enjoyed its finest hours with a set-up I had done so much to bring about, largely through the youth policy we had introduced and which had borne fruit with some magnificent home produce.

Chapter Nine

Hooked By Salmon

Having dwelt largely on the business world and the affairs of Aston Villa, I might well have created the impression that I have been a workaholic with little interest in social or leisure pursuits.

Such a conclusion would be completely erroneous as those who have shared a salmon beat with me would readily confirm. It is a fact, if also a cliché, that an escape route from daily pressures is essential for everyone, including myself. Among many other pursuits at various times, my get-away-from-it-all passion has been salmon fishing.

A consuming interest evolved from adversity. In 1960 I suffered a duodenal ulcer, the classic danger for live-on-your-nerves professional people. The ulcer burst and I ended up in hospital having five days of blood transfusions to make me strong enough to undergo an operation at the hands of a very fine surgeon, Victor Brookes. I was 'between marriages' at that time and my mother would visit me constantly, driven to the Queen Elizabeth Hospital by a friend, Sid Newey who, incidentally, had won a Bronze Medal for the steeplechase in the 1924 Olympics. On one visit he expressed the view that, to ease some of the pressures in my life, I should accompany him to his salmon fishing beat on the River Wye. Sure enough, when I was convalescing he kept his promise. On the first two occasions, nothing. But on the third visit to the lovely stretch of the River Wye in Herefordshire I landed a sixteen pound salmon. In those few minutes, just like the fish, I was hooked. Soon I was renting a stretch of the river myself at The Carrotts Beat near Hereford for two days, Sunday and Monday.

Later I had two days at Holme Lacey, still on the Wye. It was there that both my son Peter, and myself, landed thirty pounders, though he claims to this day that his was a quarter of a pound heavier than mine. Well, you've all heard these Fisherman's Tales.

From there I was a guest of Eric Haines, the well-known Birmingham butcher who owned, at one time, about 23 shops. An All-England coarse angler, he also owned the angling rights on a mile stretch of the Wye to which he gave me an open-ended invitation.

One day I was in my office in Toronto when I was invited to join a syndicate of twelve who were to contribute 1,000 Canadian dollars each to finance the searching of rivers in Newfoundland and Labrador for salmon spawning beds. About a year later we went on our first of what was to be a series of memorable salmon fishing trips to the far north of the country. We flew to Montreal and then on a further 1,000 miles to Goose Bay where we changed to a single-engine Otter seaplane and flew another 300 miles north-east.

We touched down at the mouth of the Eagle River in an area between two massive icebergs where we were met by Jack, our Eskimo-Indian ghillie.

For the uninitiated a ghillie is your guide, fishing expert and general factotum. At first we had employed him to help us to build a cabin in which we would live.

On that first visit it was all a shade rugged, believe me. The cabin was a bare structure with no heating and while there was unlimited summer sunshine by day the night temperatures were below freezing. Our shower was a suspended bucket of water with a pull cord. We were, remember, 120 miles from the nearest other dwelling and 300 miles from the 'corner shop' which was back in Goose Bay.

For ten years we undertook this annual pilgrimage and each year the accommodation, which eventually had six bedrooms, became more and more civilised. Jack married the maid, Claudette, setting up home in the annexe and they proved to be a marvellous asset in making our yearly breaks so beneficial.

As for the salmon fishing, it was simply idyllic. In the seven days our six rods would land about 250 grilse, namely young salmon returning from the sea to fresh water for the first time. The largest fish caught was about sixteen pounds, but on average they were about six pounds. To make it an 'even playing field' we all fished with three ounce, one-piece rods which meant that every catch was a little battle all of its own, with a small imitation fly on a single hook. Where we fished was beneath one of the biggest waterfalls in Canada and to see the thousands of salmon congregating there to 'jump the rapids' was a sight to behold.

One laughable little cameo sticks in mind. I was fishing on my own, up to my waders in the cold, clear water of a separate pool I had found when a noise from the bank of crashing undergrowth broke the silence. My first, rather scary reaction, was that it must be a roaming brown bear which one saw occasionally. They would rear up on their hind legs to pick berries off the trees and, when they did, they stood about six-feet tall. I once had one come along and steal the fish I had left on the bank. They were not to be treated lightly.

However, when I looked over my shoulder, I saw this character wearing plus-fours and a deerstalker hat, extremely red of face, angrily informing me that I was fishing in his private water. How he got there, in that gear, and in such a remote area I had no idea. I said: "My name's Doug Ellis, I'm from England, and I do apologise if I'm trespassing. There seemed to be no-one for miles around." He introduced himself as Dickie Hull and made it very clear he was not at all pleased at his privacy being invaded in this way. Off I went to find myself another pool and subsequently found out more about him.

The military-looking gentleman who had so invaded my isolation and solitude transpired to be very high-ranking 'military' indeed. Dickie Hull was the British Army Defence General who had made a wager with the Canadian Air Force Air Marshall that the River Dee in Scotland was more salmon-prolific than the Eagle River in Labrador. Dickie's peace-shattering appearance at 'my' pool was in pursuit of his attempt to prove his point. I can only add that, whatever his wager was, he lost it to the sheer abundance of the Labrador species.

During these marvellous trips we each had a special role to play. I had volunteered to look after our necessary food supplies. These we purchased at Goose Bay before flying out to the cabin and always I included a bottle or two of scotch and gin. Well, as I explained it was a little chilly at night.

We did, of course, live pretty much on the fish we caught, including trout. When Claudette was doing the cooking she would reprimand us for handing her fish that were far too big to get into the pan.

Lunchtimes used to be, to me, something resembling heaven on earth.

We would assemble on a little sandy bank in the middle of the river and Jack would come along in his boat to join us, bringing the drinks and a supply of ice, which was always in ready supply from the roof of the cabin.

He would light a fire of bracken and branches and inquire which were the most recent large fish to be landed. This could have been only about twenty minutes earlier. He would cut the selected specimen into large steaks which he cooked on the open fire in tin foil and the fresh fish oil, having rubbed in salt to enhance the taste.

At the fireside we would be waiting armed with large chunks of fresh bread which Claudette had baked. Believe me when you've been fishing in paradise all morning, and have teased the appetite with a couple of gin and tonics the sensation of eating the freshly cooked salmon or trout al fresco, while dipping fresh, home-baked bread in the juices all adds up to the finest meal anyone could eat. I was blessed to do so many, many times.

Eventually, however, that particular annual trip ran its course and simultaneously the beats on the River Wye were badly affected by salmon disease. The time had come to fish new waters so, in more recent years, I have been a member of a syndicate which took out a timeshare for one week each year for 99 years on the Waulkmill and Goldcastle beats on the River Tay in Scotland, where I go annually to this day.

My companions include my son Peter, Maurice Nock, ex-proprietor of the Corn Exchange restaurant in Lichfield, a Yorkshireman named John Gill, Martin Jackson and Barney Barnett. Now there's a name to conjure with. Only those who recall the TV programme *The Golden Shot* and Bob Monkhouse's famous catch-phrase 'Barney, the bolt...' will know who I mean. During our week we reckon to catch in excess of a hundred salmon having once, in the late 1980s, caught a record 188 between us. One individual who enjoyed a trip to Scotland with me was Graham Taylor, subsequently to become manager of Aston Villa and then England. When he came up to try his hand at the sport I gave him a little tuition and off he went in a boat for the day with our ghillie. He was a total beginner, remember.

Usually this would result in a rather disappointing nil return. But not for Graham. He came in with an amazing FIVE salmon, all of which he had caught himself. When you consider that thousands of fishermen go for years without landing that many in total it was some feat. Naturally, as one would expect, he claimed that it was a result of pure skill. Me? I reckon he was a lucky beggar.

Graeme Souness was another to try his hand with us, when he was manager of Rangers in Glasgow. Graeme had never caught a fish in his life but confessed to having seen his father poach one, not an unusual occurrence in Scotland. Like Graham Taylor he was given some basic tuition, having been roused at 6.30 am, and sent off in the boat with the ghillie to a favourable spot.

Less than half-an-hour later they were back, Graeme having caught a seventeen pounder. He was white as a sheet and dripping in perspiration.

It turned out that his exhausted appearance was more down to euphoria than fatigue, though he could not believe the strength of the fish in 'resisting arrest'.

The local press were informed of the Rangers manager's catch and one of the reporters inquired of his greatest sporting moment, was it scoring a goal for Scotland or landing his salmon? "Catching that bloody fish..." he told them, or words to that effect.

Jimmy Greaves also joined me on a salmon fishing expedition in Scotland, though he came to make a TV programme which many readers may recall having seen. We took him to a rock about four feet square in the middle of the river, with water raging around him, but as we were pulling away in our boat so that he could be filmed in isolation he was pleading in a frightened voice: "Don't leave me. I can't swim..." Anyway after a while, with a little help, he hooked a fish and was handed The Priest, which is a special truncheon to kill the salmon quickly and avoid any suffering. He simply looked aghast at the suggestion. "I couldn't do that," he insisted as I took The Priest from him to deliver the fatal, stunning blow.

There is a lovely moment, on the film, where he is looking at me out of the corner of his eye and saying to the others: "See, I told you Doug was deadly." Salmon fishing in Ireland, where I got to enjoy the company of Jackie Charlton, has also provided rich memories, though a horse racing episode springs strongly to mind.

Back in 1958 I had taken out a 21-year lease on the travel agency office in Grafton Street, Dublin, operating package deal holidays under the banner of Sunflight and Global. Later I opened another in North Street, Belfast, for similar purposes.

On one occasion, around 1962-63, when I visited the Irish Derby at the Curragh with the trainer Aubrey Brabazon, I was accommodated in the Jockey Hall, all very basic and open-ended like stables. Anyone who has visited the Irish Derby will confirm that the party goes on nearly all night.

I gave in around 3am and was awakened at about 7.30 when a face appeared above the half-door and said in that lovely Irish lilt: "Your horse is ready for you to see, Mr Ellis." "Horse? What flippin' horse?" "The one you bought last night, Mr Ellis." "I never bought a horse last night. Did I...?" Anyway I scrambled up and took a look at the horse, liked it very much and agreed to buy it for £2,000. A spot of kidology on their part had turned out for real and though they offered me a get out, by now I was sold on the idea. The two-year-old was renamed 'Sunflight' and we ran it in claret-and-blue colours, sadly without winning a bean, in five races. It should have been an expensive hobby by now yet I was receiving no bills from Aubrey Brabazon in the entire five months of ownership. Then I received a telephone call from him. He had some Malaysians interested in buying the horse and was advising me to sell and to leave the details to him.

This I agreed, and when I eventually did receive an invoice it was a little Irish classic in its own right. On one side were the registration fee, the vet's bills, the training fees and so on. On the other side was the income from the sale... and I ended up out of pocket, by one shilling, on the entire deal. I don't imagine the Irish lads 'lost' much, either.

Thus, I didn't win a single race in Ireland and didn't catch many salmon but we did OK for footballers, with Steve Staunton, Paul McGrath, Andy Townsend, Ray Houghton, Gareth Farrelly and the like dating right back to Con Martin of the early post-war years.

Also we have an active Villa fan club out there. If Villa Park is my second home I would readily adopt Ireland as my second country.

While salmon fishing has been a source of great pleasure and relaxation in my life another pursuit I have tried, namely skiing, proved only to be a pain in the neck.

As a family we would sometimes visit the famous resort of Kitzbühel for winter sports, but while Heidi, Simon and Oliver became excellent skiers, life on the slopes proved difficult for me. In contrast to their being perfectly competent for the more difficult Black Route I would confine myself to the far safer Blue Route and I well remember my last descent. The day before we were to return home our two sons, teenagers as they were then, persuaded me to try the Black Route on the assurance that they would stay with me and safely escort me down. Off we went and for a while I was managing OK when Simon and Oliver, in typical teenager fashion, forgot their undertaking and left me trailing behind in order to display their own expertise. Overnight there had been a particularly heavy frost and the surface of the slope was even more treacherous than usual.

Try as I did I just could not get any grip once my speed had picked up. Soon I was more or less out of control and heading downhill fast.

Alberto Tomba I was not. Heaven knows how fast it was, probably very slow by skiing standards, but to me it felt like about 70mph. In order to feel safer I was crouched on my haunches negotiating my own version of the slalom when I noticed ahead of me a little hollow with a rising slope behind it. If I could steer into that hollow then the slope at the back would pull me up. Or so I thought. Wrongly it transpired. Into the hollow I went... and straight over the top of the rising slope, as though in some comedy film, to end up headfirst in a tangled heap and momentarily unconscious.

There I was found by an Austrian lady skier who kindly helped me down the Blue Route, where I ought to have been in the first place. The outcome of that little episode was seventeen days in the Priory Hospital with a cracked vertebra in my neck. That ended any passing fancy I'd ever had for skiing. As I say, even recalling this story is a pain in the neck.

Because of the neck injury I was warned to avoid certain activities, like diving into the water, though I have to confess that, when out on my boat, sometimes the temptation has been too great. Medical advice has been ignored more than once.

Talking of boats I do recall spending a particular day with the England party anchored in the Mediterranean off Sardinia during Italia 90. The players were skylarking on the deck and Gazza, being Gazza, decided that since we had a Bull (namely Steve) in the party he would complete the scenario by acting out the role of matador. Gazza had Bully charging at him, head down, as they gave a mock display of bull fighting. Gazza would playfully take the head-down charges on his body.

However as Bully warmed to his impersonation of a beast of the same name Gazza waited for him to make his most ferocious charge yet before executing a true matador's side-step for Bully's rush to take him headlong into the sea to howls of approval from their England colleagues.

Chapter Ten

Buying Back From Bendall

Every professional person has a profit and loss account in their career, whoever they may be, and I am well aware that one of the 'debits' against my name in the eyes of some observers has always been that the greatest trophies were won during my absence.

Historically and factually this is perfectly accurate. In the three years between 1979 and 1982, when I had little connection with Aston Villa FC other than as a continuing supporter, the Championship and the European Cup were won. The Super Cup was won after my return in 1982-83.

I do not attempt to gloss over these details which are there in the record books. Indeed, in one way, and without attempting to steal anyone else's glory, I remain rather proud of them.

To appreciate why I feel pride rather than embarrassment in the reality that these momentous achievements came during my absence, one has merely to recall the state of the club at the time of what has been called the '1968 Revolution' and the transformation which had gradually taken place. Only by that rescue act of 1968 and all the progress made in the following ten years or so could Aston Villa FC have become champions of their country and their continent.

Also, I categorically maintain, that these major successes were brought about with the very club set-up and managerial staff which had been initiated by the board during that period.

What better example of this could there have been than the influential role played in the successes by the young players Gordon Cowans and

Gary Shaw, from the youth scheme we had set up. The captain, Dennis Mortimer, was also from those earlier years.

To the day I die it will remain my firm conviction that Aston Villa would have won those trophies had I been allowed to remain as chairman or simply on the board. What's more, I humbly submit, the club would have continued in a far more stable financial state than it did during those three years and for a while afterwards.

The fact is that internal instability was constantly caused by Ron Saunders' incessant involvement in power politics of the 'divide and conquer' variety I have described earlier, namely setting one director off against another and thus encouraging splits to emerge.

Another firm conviction of mine is that had Ron concentrated on his outstanding strength, that of building trophy-winning football teams, we could have achieved for Aston Villa much of what Alex Ferguson and a supportive board have since achieved for Manchester United.

Instead he was significantly instrumental in my departure from the club and, during that time, remember, success on the field went side-by-side with lack of continuity behind the scenes.

There were several changes of chairman and other directors in a period of less than ten years, mostly during Saunders' term as manager between 1974-82. I was not the only one who had difficulty with him, believe me.

Even during the successful European Cup campaign there were on-going problems between manager and board, notably the roll-over contract dispute which finally led to his own sensational walk-out.

That particular episode remains etched in my mind for the amusing way in which I first got wind of it.

Not far from where I live on Four Oaks estate was the original home of Keith Coombs, the chairman of Birmingham City who by then had moved to Knowle.

Before he changed residence his gardener and my own were friends and, like all staff anywhere the world over, would have their little chats about their job and the household for whom they worked.

When Keith moved house and district he retained the services of his gardener who thus travelled from his home in Sutton Coldfield and back each day and kept in contact with his mate who was employed by myself.

One day during this period my gardener was able to inform me that, while Ron Saunders was still at Villa Park, he had been seen entering Keith Coombs's residence in Knowle.

Consequently when the shock-horror of his departure from Villa Park and the 'surprise' of his joining Birmingham City as replacement for Jim Smith hit the headlines I must have been one of the very few football enthusiasts who was not in the least surprised. My gardener had kept me well posted!

However, soon afterwards a newspaper headline that not only did surprise me, but also annoyed me intensely, appeared in a local newspaper stating that Ron Bendall, the then Aston Villa chairman, was to sell his shares in the club to Harry Parkes.

Over my dead body...!

In next to no time the lines from Four Oaks to the Isle of Man, where the Bendall family lived, were humming loud and clear.

"What about our agreement when you purchased my shares three years ago," I asked him. "You promised that you would give me first refusal to buy them back at par and we shook hands on it..."

To give him his due he accepted that we did have such a gentleman's agreement though, typical of the shrewd financial operator, he pulled a fast one on me despite 'honouring' that agreement.

"You can have them if you pay the same as Mr Parkes has agreed to pay," he replied. "If you do that I will honour my commitment to you."

"You're on," I said, and was on the next suitable flight to the Isle of Man where I booked into a hotel not far from where he lived.

The shareholding involved was just less than forty per cent of the total share capital of the club, namely the controlling element. When Ron Bendall and I met next day he told me the price that Harry Parkes had offered to pay him. In return I offered him one pound more, which he accepted and, with professional witnesses whom I insisted should be present, the deal was done.

Bearing in mind the manner of my departure in 1979 I took a measure of satisfaction from the belief that I had out-negotiated one of my previous rivals by the princely sum of one pound. This banknote, incidentally, I suggested to Ron Bendall, ought to be framed and displayed by him as a reminder of the day he sold Aston Villa to the highest bidder, by one pound.

Little did I know that there was still a twist to come in this particular story. It was only when I met Harry Parkes later, and we discussed what had taken place, that I discovered that Mr Bendall had over-quoted to me the actual figure by £80,000. Harry produced for me copies of three

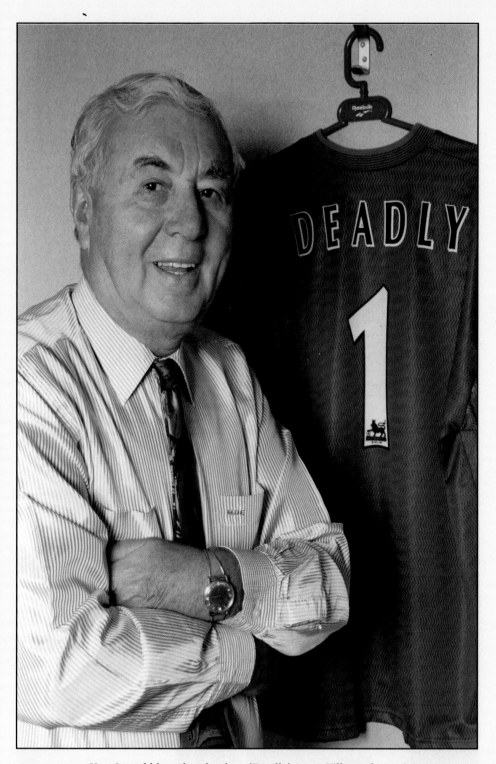

How I would have loved to be a 'Deadly' Aston Villa goalscorer!

ABOVE - Business premises in Birmingham, where sunshine, package-deal holidays were pioneered.

LEFT - Dancing with Heidi 'my beautiful bride'.

TOP LEFT - A post-World War 1 toddler, brought up by a widowed mother... and World War II service in the Fleet Air Arm.

LEFT - My mother Jane and my two sons, Oliver and Simon.

ABOVE - "Now listen here, Deadly...." Jimmy Greaves, who was responsible for landing me with the nickname, cheekily takes the chair.

LEFT - "How's that for soccer style?" John Gidman can't believe his eyes.

FAR LEFT - *A fisherman's tale, but with evidence to prove a record catch.*

ABOVE - *It's a big 'un, but don't go overboard.*

LEFT - *I'm not throwing that one back!*

BELOW - *Afloat with Villa. Deadly prepares to set sail from Palma, Majorca.*

Bathtime at Old Trafford. Football League Cup Final triumph, second replay against Everton, 1977 and Ray Graydon finds an unorthodox way of 'sharing' his bottle of bubbly. The celebratory soaking did nothing to improve my new, expensive Italian mohair suit!

LEFT - Dr Deadly, at your service and an honorary degree from Central England University.

BELOW - The League Cup comes 'home' to Villa Park, again, this time courtesy of a magnificent 3-1 victory over Manchester United by Ron Atkinson's team in 1994.

RIGHT - Rubbing shoulders with world celebrities... South Africa's President, Nelson Mandela... The Princess Royal... John Major when he was Prime Minister.

Meeting some of my football heroes...

LEFT - Tom 'Pongo' Waring, great pre-war Villa goalscorer.

RIGHT - Paul 'Macca' McGrath, one of Aston Villa's greatest signings, who kindly provided the Foreword to this book.

RIGHT - My mate Tom Finney, now Sir Tom, a special guest at my surprise 70th birthday party.

BELOW - the one and only Sir Stanley Matthews.

10 DOWNING STREET
LONDON SW1A 2AA

THE PRIME MINISTER

It can be said of few people that they have left an indelible impression on their chosen walk of life. There is no question that Doug Ellis is one of those few. He joined Aston Villa when memories of England's success in the 1966 World Cup were still fresh in our minds. Our national team's fortunes may have waned since then, but Doug has helped take Villa from success to success in the years since then. Today it is in the first rank of professional soccer teams in Britain.

His many friends, and all the supporters of Aston Villa everywhere, will want to join me in wishing Doug many happy returns for his 70th birthday, and congratulations on reaching his quarter century at the helm of "the Villans".

John Major

November 1993

cheques comprising his total offer, with two associates, to prove that I had been duped by a canny financial operator.

There was I believing that I had outbid my rival for the club by a mere one pound when it turned out to be £80,001. To be fair, though, I had resecured approximately forty per cent of Aston Villa FC and I certainly was not complaining about the cost.

The one thing I had wanted, professionally, since my departure was to get back to Villa Park and carry on the all-round development of one of the greatest names in football. Now the door was open for this to be achieved. In this context a sum of £80,000 was incidental.

However, the biggest 'plus' of all was that in my second term I could bring into being the principles I had learned at St Andrew's, namely that a board of directors all pulling in the same direction is essential for on-going progress. Things would be very, very different in my second term which, at the time of writing has continued for fifteen harmonious years. There has been no more wrangling, no more destructive disputes, thanks to colleagues who keep any differences of opinion, and there are some, to the boardroom table.

At the start of the story I described the state of Villa's affairs in December 1968. In 1982 I returned to a ground which now had a North Stand replacing the old Witton terraces (a project I had been instrumental in starting before my departure) while, on the field of course, the team had been champions of England and Europe.

Sounds cosy all round, doesn't it? Reality, sad to say, was slightly different. There is a figure burned deep into my brain of £1.8m in actual and hidden debts that existed at the club. A whole pile of bills were in the 'in' tray still to be settled on the new stand, firms who had supplied services had not been paid, there were stories circulating of 'missing' funds, though I never had actual evidence of this, and the whole atmosphere seemed to be one of suspicion. I will not dwell on this unhappy state of affairs, the subject is covered in detail in the book: *Villa Park - 100 Years*, other than to observe that Aston Villa FC did not possess the feeling one would expect in a club which has been well-managed behind the scenes, bearing in mind the outstanding success on the field.

Sadly also, by now, playing affairs were not as healthy as one would have expected, either. Certainly it seemed to me that the opportunity to use the trophy successes as a springboard to further glories had already been wasted.

The manager when I returned to the club was Tony Barton, who had been Ron Saunders' assistant, largely with 'chief scout' duties.

Tony was a very nice, well-meaning and professional man who had been an absolutely first-class talent-spotter at first-team level. Many of the excellent signings made during Saunders' reign were down to Tony. Anyone who knew Ron at the time will tell you that he hardly ever went to watch players himself. Just as Saunders' strength was in turning sets of players into well-prepared teams, so Tony's was in finding the players with the necessary qualities.

Tony sadly died later with heart trouble and I will simply say of him that I did not feel that he was the right person to take the club forward in the long term. I had a good deal of criticism over his dismissal but, like all those people in executive positions, I had to do what I thought was right at the time.

Looking back now I guess it was in that period between May 1984 and May 1987 that I acquired the nickname 'Deadly', pinned upon me in jocular fashion by Jimmy Greaves because of these managerial changes, or maybe because of my expertise in stunning a salmon!

There were three managers dismissed during this extremely mediocre spell for the club, namely Tony Barton, Graham Turner and Billy McNeill MBE. From Champions in 1981 Villa had slipped to 11th, 6th and 10th and average gates had declined from 33,000 to 21,000. We felt that a new direction was required and I have to confess, in retrospect, for those first three years we did not get it right.

In order to replace Tony Barton we advertised for applicants, a short-list was drawn up, and Graham Turner was appointed. I had admired his work as player-manager of Shrewsbury Town, on a shoestring budget and the board was impressed with the man when we interviewed him.

My feelings were that we had found someone who could develop into a top name, in the same way as previous young managers had emerged around the country. Finding the next great manager while that individual is still in his embryo stage is like discovering a rough diamond, one of the greatest services any board of directors could provide for its club.

We tried to do so, with the best of motives, in appointing Graham Turner, but unfortunately his weakness proved to be that of lack of First Division experience and know-how. This probably worked against him in the eyes of some of his experienced players.

Graham did an honest, hard-working job for the club but without making the necessary breakthrough he required into the big league. He finished tenth in his first season, then 16th and was struggling when he departed in the September of his third season. Consequently, we were back to square one in terms of finding a manager of the necessary calibre to take the club forward.

This time we were deeply conscious of the fact that lack of experience in the major leagues had worked against Graham Turner. Now supporters were calling for someone who possessed this experience in abundance.

Again we advertised and this time Billy McNeill, the then manager of Manchester City, appeared to be the ideal person. Billy, like Graham Turner before him, was a likeable, amiable individual, but with the important difference that he had won a record number of medals in Scottish football with Celtic, was an ex-Scottish international centre half and European Cup-winner.

His contribution to Scottish football had been honoured with an MBE in the Queen's Birthday Honours List in 1974 and he saw the huge opportunity of the job at Villa Park. Once again, however, practice did not match the theory and he was unable to check the slide initiated under his predecessor and we were relegated in 22nd place at the end of 1986-87.

Here it is only fair to point out that, while we attempted to fund the purchase of players, attendances had been at a poor level and the club had not been found in a happy state financially despite the successes of the early-1980s. Resources for massive purchasing in the transfer market simply were not there.

A look at the annual profit or losses on trading during this period is revealing: 1979 (loss) £150,000; 1980 (loss) £679,000; 1981 (profit) £203,000; 1982 (profit) £311,000; 1983 (loss) £53,251; 1984 (11 months to May, profit) £263,426.

These figures show that finances had been heading downward after the two major trophy successes, thus the first priority had been to reverse the trend, memories of 1968 and all that still fairly fresh in mind!

By now I had truly been through the mill in football both as a director and as a chairman, 'helped' in a strange way by a fleeting connection with Wolverhampton Wanderers during my three years absence from Villa Park. Quite candidly it would have been better had I not allowed myself to get involved in any way. Hindsight is a wonderful science...!

Basically, I was invited by the late John Wardle, senior partner in the solicitors firm of Edge & Ellison, to have lunch with him and Sydney

Shore, a high-ranking executive of Lloyds Bank whom he had also invited. When we reached the coffee stage, Mr Shore asked if, since I was no longer on the board of Aston Villa, would I be interested in taking over at Wolves?

At that stage not only had I no idea of the extent of the financial problems at Molineux, I had been approached to one extent or another by five football clubs who were seeking new directors able to make cash injections. I will not name the clubs concerned since the talks were strictly confidential and possibly some of those involved are still connected with those clubs but I did visit three of them, purely in an advisory capacity.

My first reaction to the Lloyds Bank approach was, similar to the other five, namely that my allegiance was still to Aston Villa FC and I was quite reluctant to consider joining any other club. That's where the matter seemed to have ended until, a few weeks later, I received another call from John Wardle saying that Sydney Shore wished to return his lunch invitation, at the bank boardroom in Colmore Row, Birmingham, and that again I was included. This time the topic of Wolves arrived at the 'second' stage and, in a weak moment I guess, I agreed to visit Lloyds branch in Wolverhampton with Mr Shore.

By now the position had emerged that Wolves were in a state bordering on bankruptcy and their affairs were in the hands of the bank. The 'financial rescue' experiences I had gleaned at Aston Villa in 1968 were clearly regarded as the necessary qualifications for some sort of similar salvage operation at Molineux.

Things were certainly very bad. The team was sliding towards relegation from Division One and debts were mounting.

The reason for Lloyds Bank's persistence in wishing to appoint a new chairman and to strengthen the board was to avoid the other alternative. This would have been for the bank to call in the receivers to close the club down, a move which would have alienated supporters, not a move they relished bearing in mind the affection for the club in the region and the number of prestige customers on their books who would have been mortified by such a turn of events.

When I arrived for the meeting in Wolverhampton Mr Shore had also invited two Wolverhampton Wanderers directors. At this meeting I accepted the chairmanship of the club on the understanding that my friend Malcolm Finlayson was also brought in as a director.

Malcolm, a former fine Scottish-born goalkeeper for the club, had made more than 200 appearances for Wolves between 1956 and 1964 and after his playing days he had become a successful businessman and multi-millionaire, owning several factories in the Black Country.

Another condition I made was that I brought in my own chartered accountants, with all costs being met by Lloyds Bank. On June 16th, 1982, the then chairman, Harry Marshall, resigned and I replaced him.

In the event, our new regime at Molineux survived for only about ten days, as I recall. The figures produced by my accountants revealed Wolverhampton Wanderers to be hopelessly and irretrievably bankrupt.

I note in an official club history that debts were said to be £2.5m, a huge figure in those days and £500,000 more than originally believed. 'The cost of the new Molineux Stand had become a millstone' it adds. It is also interesting to recall that, before Ian Greaves took the ill-fated Wolves managerial job, a certain Alex Ferguson, the then manager of Aberdeen, had been approached, but in vain. In retrospect, Alex wasn't a bad judge in waiting for the Manchester United offer to arrive.

However, by company law directors cannot continue to run a company which is insolvent. We had no alternative but to put the proud club, which had been founded in 1877, into receivership. Now, remember, it was not Lloyds Bank who were 'responsible' for this but the new board under Doug Ellis.

By this move the club was saved from extinction by just twenty-four hours (again as reported in the club's official history) and subsequently a survival package was accepted from the Bhatti brothers-backed Derek Dougan consortium and a new company was formed.

All this confirms that, as I wrote earlier, by the time I returned as chairman of Aston Villa I had learned a thing or three about the necessity of keeping a football club's finances in good order, though the component parts did not begin to bear fruit until we appointed Graham Taylor to succeed Billy McNeill in July 1987.

Chapter Eleven

How We Nearly Lost David Platt

Let's get back to this nickname of mine, 'Deadly Doug' that, oddly, took on a new lease of life when Brian Little, against my wishes, decided that he would resign for reasons of his own and under no pressure whatsoever to do so.

I'm not resentful about the nickname 'Deadly', having explained that it was partly down, anyway, to my ability to stun a salmon. Nor am I reluctant to discuss it. Likewise, to complete the picture, I am not filled with remorse that I have been responsible for firing seven managers during my terms as chairman. I have no qualms at all about the principle that if a manager fails he pays the price with his job.

One aspect of it that does irritate me rather, though, is that newspapers come up with a list of eleven managers over whom I have 'presided', leaving the impression that I have fired the other ten which, of course, is not the case. The reality is that seven have been dismissed in my term of some twenty-seven years. Arthur Cox was no more than caretaker manager and this was before I became chairman, Ron Saunders, whom I had appointed, left the club of his own free will when I wasn't there, two others, Graham Taylor and Brian Little, have left voluntarily while a third, Jo Venglos, had expressed himself as more than willing to resign before we mutually agreed to his leaving.

The departure of any manager from a major club is, naturally, a news item of great public interest but it does occur to me that the newspapers who make the procedure all sound so heartless probably fire more top executives in twelve months than I have dismissed in twenty-seven years, and with a lesser cheque in their hand than we have frequently provided, to soften the blow.

The fact is that managers know the name of the game when they accept a managerial appointment. The rules are clear enough. They MUST bring about progress in playing affairs during the period of their contract. If such progress is not being made after a respectable period of time, then an agreement is reached over the unexpired portion, and they leave.

Generally speaking, a manager gets the praise for success. A chairman gets the flak for failure. He is left with one option if he wants to improve things. Basically, the board's job is the welfare and financial health of the club and keeping its facilities up to scratch, the manager's responsibility is results and the supporter is the most important cog of all. I never forget these guidelines.

I've frequently been accused of dwelling too much on balancing the books, a charge that I find unacceptable. Anyone wishing to play Fantasy Football can do so in the newspapers. In the real world you only get what you pay for in real money, not make-believe.

All I ask is for my record as the head of what is after all a football-business enterprise to be judged by the official figures published at the time of the 1997 flotation. I will happily be assessed in this way if managers agree to be judged equally on their own results.

Of all the 15 clubs who floated up to a similar time to ourselves in 1997, Aston Villa's was the best balance sheet, with a proven record of profitability over a ten year period. The actual profit figure was £23m with a net deficiency on transfers of nearly £11m, leaving a net profit carried forward of £12m. I submit this background as a fertile one against which a manager can operate and if he fails to bring success then he is responsible.

I never, ever interfere with training, fitness, tactics, team selection or a manager's relationship with the media. On the other hand I never hesitate to give my opinion on players whom we might sign to strengthen our squad. Whenever I see a player whom I consider to be of the right quality, then I make it known to the manager for his consideration.

A case in point was when Brazil played Sweden at Villa Park in the Umbro Cup competition in the summer of 1995. I was so impressed with Juninho and Roberto Carlos that I sounded out the Brazilian president about them and he expressed the view that Carlos could be available. I invited the player to the boardroom and, though rather nervous, he said he was very impressed with the club and the facilities of the stadium and would be interested in joining us. The Brazilian president acted as interpreter for us and it emerged that the player would accept a contract with us, paid in American dollars, at a rate that was no higher than our highest-paid players of that time. He indicated that he would be interested in having a further meeting with us back home in Brazil but, unfortunately, Brian Little was less enthusiastic than myself and thus we did not pursue the deal.

Since then I have watched with interest on TV his wonderful displays for Real Madrid and noted with even greater interest reports linking him with Manchester United and mind-blowing multi-million pound contracts and fees being talked about. Whenever I see Roberto Carlos, on TV, bending free-kicks around walls of defenders and scoring sensational goals for the Spanish club I must confess to reminiscing about that meeting in our boardroom and thinking 'If only I had insisted...'

However, I would always respect the manager's right to make his own player selections, while managers in turn have to take board decisions on finance.

To my knowledge top managers have never been poorly paid and in the increasingly lucrative world of the FA Premiership they receive up to three and four times that of the Prime Minister whom, I believe, gets around £150,000 per year.

No, I do not object to being called 'Deadly Doug' when I dismiss a manager, especially since contracts are carefully honoured.

However, at this point I readily hold up my hands and confess that neither of the two appointments I had made during my second term as chairman had been successful. I take some of the responsibility for having selected them in the first place.

To be fair to Graham Turner and Billy McNeill they served the club during a period when it was necessary to exert the most prudent financial policies because I would never preside over any organisation that was allowing itself to fall deeper and deeper into debt.

The bottom line of all this was that in the summer of 1987 it was absolutely essential that we appointed a proven, experienced manager who could steer the club back into the First Division quickly and while so doing point the way towards further steady improvements.

One name that found favour with a section of the public was Ron

Atkinson who by then had been dismissed by Manchester United despite twice winning the FA Cup for them. Ron was one of the possibles I had in mind myself but then, among the has-beens, up-and-comers and no-chance merchants who apply for every managerial vacancy that arises I opened an unexpected letter that changed everything.

It was from a gentleman named Dick Taylor, himself a former Aston Villa manager who originally came to the club as Joe Mercer's assistant in December 1958 and succeeded Joe as boss himself in May 1967 when affairs at Villa Park were heading for an all-time low. After leaving Villa Park Dick, now deceased, started a sports outfitters business not far from the ground and soon took over the role of equipment suppliers to the club.

Dick's ever-smiling face could frequently be seen at Bodymoor Heath or Villa Park as he became friendly with the successive managers, players and staff who could always rely on a generous discount on his goods. I feel sure that he performed the excellent service for the club at a minimal profit for himself.

During his playing days, at Scunthorpe and Grimsby, Dick had been a friend of Graham Taylor's sports writer father, Tom, who covered Scunthorpe for the local Evening Telegraph. True to Dick's caring manner he had always kept an eye on Tommy's lad's career and was thus in regular contact with Graham, then manager at Watford, to where he subsequently returned to be later re-united with Elton John as his chairman.

The football world at large would probably have believed that Graham, having put down some fairly deep roots at the club over ten years of magnificent progress, would stay at Vicarage Road for life.

Not so. The letter I opened from Dick Taylor said that his mate Tommy Taylor's lad, was ready to move on and that the challenge of managing a major club like Aston Villa was just what he was seeking.

As soon as I read Dick's letter my reaction was: 'Yes, yes, yes...'

To be totally fair to the last two managers it had not been easy for them. Transfer resources had been limited. To some degree they had needed to help generate their own team-rebuilding resources by wheeling and dealing.

A kick-start was required to get the club's playing affairs moving forward. They had not been able to provide it. Now I felt I knew a man who could: Graham Taylor.

He became my one and only candidate and though it took a good deal of negotiation through his representative who meticulously formulated the nuts and bolts of his contract, he was appointed manager in July 1987.

By comparison with what Graham had been earning at Watford it was a very good deal worked out by his representative and myself. The attention to detail, paid on Graham's behalf, told me a lot about him. This proved to be one of his great strengths in that nothing was knowingly left to chance. His organisational ability was absolutely excellent.

Obviously Graham's was a very high-profile appointment, announced to a packed press conference at Villa Park. Certainly there was no hiding the reality that Graham's brief, if possible, was to get the club back into the First Division at the first attempt. A tough assignment, indeed, and the players had to know he meant business. Graham's first meeting with the players, after I had introduced them to him, sticks in my mind for a particular reason.

One of the first things he did was to ask them collectively if any of them had any problems, any complaints, any desire to leave the club, anything at all they wished to discuss with him because his policy as a manager would be that of honest relationships. Everything must be out in the open to start as they meant to go on.

There was a complete silence from the group. So Graham asked again with a similar negative response. Then, turning to Tony Dorigo, he said: "Well I understand that Chelsea want to sign you and that you want to go..." Everyone knew it was true. Dorigo could only meekly agree that this was the case.

Thus within minutes Graham had got his message across. "Don't try to pull the wool over my eyes lads, because I know the score..." This 'don't-mess-me-about' attitude and his attention to detail quickly became highly respected by his players. I recall he had a notice on his desk saying: 'Thank you for not smoking in my office'. Nobody ever did. He hated the habit. At one time managers would allow smoking on the team coach. Graham jumped on that, straightaway.

However, Dorigo was sold to Chelsea and in that first season the fee helped to fund relatively inexpensive signings such as Kevin Gage, Steve Sims, Alan McInally, Andy Gray and Stuart Gray. This was, of course, the 'other' Andy Gray, but mention of the name reminds me of when we re-signed the original one, now the BSkyB analyst, from Everton in 1985. That was some experience in itself. Graham Turner, then the manager, was on holiday so he asked me to complete the signing, a task that proved to be far less simple than it sounded. The process necessitated my finding Andy who was also on holiday, somewhere along Portugal's Algarve. Somewhere. But where?

Despite inquiries among all his friends we were unable to obtain either a holiday address or a telephone number for him. All we knew was that he was in a private bungalow with his ex-Wolves playing colleague, Kenny Hibbitt, and their respective wives. I flew down to Faro with his friend, and subsequently his agent, Dave Ismay, who now works for the club in charge of Special Projects. Fortunately, being in the travel industry, I had former staff resident on the Algarve and they were commissioned to check Andy's whereabouts with each hotel and travel agent along the famous eighty-mile stretch of coastline.

As a result of the search, and within forty-eight hours, Dave and I were able to arrive, quite unannounced, at a particular villa on the edge of the beach. I can still imagine the expressions on the faces of the little party who were enjoying themselves around their private swimming pool when David and I appeared around the corner of the building. They just couldn't believe how anyone could have tracked them down to such an isolated hideaway when they had left no forwarding address with anyone.

However, I had taken a blank contract with me and, after a brief negotiation, Andy agreed to return to Villa Park, whereupon we all adjourned for an excellent meal at a fish restaurant near the beach. The next day, I understand, the president and manager of the Dutch club Feyenoord wanted to sign him and were standing by with his private jet, but they were twenty-fours too late. That's if they could have found him...

However, back to Graham Taylor's reign as manager.

Our start under him in Division Two, with a rather fragmented squad, was not encouraging, namely draw, defeat, defeat, draw. In fact, looking back at the records now, I see we won but one of our opening seven Second Division matches.

No-one doubted that Graham Taylor had a big job to do as the football fraternity watched to see whether he truly could operate at a major club as he had done in taking Watford from the lower reaches to Wembley and into Europe. Gradually, the answer unfolded positively as results improved. However, as they did, another 'star' player problem arrived as it became clear that Mark Walters wanted to move on.

Mark, an outstanding local lad who was born close to Villa Park, was firmly on the England international ladder as one of the most naturally talented young players in the country. We suspected that Everton who, under Howard Kendall had won the Championship in season 1986-87, were letting it be known that they would like to sign him and that this knowledge was making Mark unsettled at Villa Park.

Sure enough an approach arrived, followed by an offer and negotiations for a fee of £550,000, which I felt was too low for such a player, especially as we had our suspicions at how the first approach had been made.

What followed was a chain of events which Everton knew nothing about and which resulted in Mark Walters joining a different club for a fee of £50,000 higher. I made a telephone call to Graeme Souness, then manager of Rangers in Glasgow and someone whom I knew socially, having salmon-fished with him.

"Do us a little favour, Graeme", I asked him, knowing that as an ex-Liverpool player he would not mind us putting a little pressure on Everton.

"Make it known in the Glasgow press that you are interested in signing Mark Walters for £650,000." The reason for this, I explained, was that I didn't think Everton had gone about things in the right way and were getting the player a touch too cheaply.

Graeme agreed and then telephoned me back to ask: "Who is this player, Mark Walters? Do I know him?" When I filled him in with a run-down on Mark, Graeme remarked: "We're looking for a player like that. Can we talk to him?" Sure, they could!

My next task was to get Mark's agent to make sure that, before the player signed at Goodison Park, he was made aware that Graeme Souness wanted to talk to him at Ibrox. This we succeeded in doing and Mark told Everton he would think over their offer but that he also intended to talk to Rangers. In the meantime Graeme Souness did his homework on Walters, realised what a quality player he was and made him a contract offer he couldn't refuse. That left the small matter of the fee. 'How much do want?' Graeme asked me.

"You know the price", I replied. "It's £650,000..." There was a disbelieving pause. "Surely you're not holding me to that price", he remonstrated. "Everton were only paying £550,000. You rang me to do you a favour." I couldn't argue with that so we compromised on £600,000. Mark Walters went to Ibrox Park instead of Goodison and Aston Villa banked another £50,000 to assist Graham Taylor's team rebuilding plans.

And very successful they were, too. To confirm this I have merely to think of the name 'David Platt' and to recall another episode from the past which remains etched in my mind. First, let me say that Graham Taylor was always cheerful in his manner, extremely calm and courteous in all his dealings and careful about what he said. An even-tempered sort of person. With this description in mind you can imagine the impact when, one day, he burst into my office like a totally different individual to the one I had come to know.

He was absolutely incensed. "That bastard Steve Harrison", he blurted out. "He's stabbed me in the back over David Platt..." Steve Harrison had been Graham's number two at Villa Park but had left to become manager at Watford. Steve, according to Graham, had been privy to the knowledge that Villa wanted to sign Platt from Crewe, and were intending to do so.

Graham had been systematically watching Platt and doing his homework on his character. As a result he was convinced that here was a ripe plum in the transfer market waiting to be plucked from a club who would not be able to refuse a reasonable offer.

I could understand this simmering anger in Graham that I had not witnessed before. His feelings were that he had looked after Steve as a player, helped him into the coaching side, brought him to an outstanding job at Villa Park and then released him from his contract so that he could return to Watford as manager.

Yet here he was using that help to steal away a signing which was to be one of the most inspired made by any manager at any time. He had naturally confided in Steve about the conversations he'd had with the manager of Crewe, Dario Gradi, thus putting him in an ideal position to make a bid himself.

Before this outburst took place I had been quietly advised by contacts in the directors' guest room at a match to 'go and get this boy, Platt', so I personally had confirmation that the proposed signing was a sensible one.

"He (Steve Harrison) knew all about my talks with Crewe", added Graham. "I had offered £175,000 and he (Harrison) has gone in behind my back and agreed a deal at £200,000."

My obvious reaction to Graham's annoyance was to ask him what he intended to do about it. "Nothing", he said. "If that's the way they want to work, they can get on with it." Fortunately, without having suffered the irritation that had so got to Graham, I was able to see the situation a little differently.

"Look", I said. "You've done your homework, you've had all the recommendations, I've had a recommendation myself. Don't give up on him. Get in your car, get up the M6, go in and offer £225,000." If I recall correctly Graham's words to me were: "Do you really mean that, Chairman. I don't like it. It's against my principles." He felt he had done a deal at £175,000 and didn't feel inclined to be gazumped by his own mate into offering more. Before or after I have never seen Graham Taylor so agitated as he was on that occasion, even when he was prowling the touchline in the famous film of the World Cup qualifier that ended his career as England manager.

In contrast I had no such reservations about upping the price for such a promising young player. "Go and sign him", I said. And he did. Had I been Steve Harrison's chairman I would probably have been equally enthusiastic about his enterprise in attempting to sign such a bargain! Strange how football works out. Steve was, of course, John Gregory's choice as his first-team coach to return to Villa Park from Preston where he worked at that time. We were more than pleased to welcome him back. No hard feelings about his trying to 'steal' David Platt from under our nose. Football is a competitive business.

Platt, whom Graham declined to pigeon hole when the press quizzed him about the type of role he would play, went on to appear in eleven of the final twelve matches of our promotion campaign to play a most valuable part in our returning to the First Division in one season. Graham always insisted that Platt wasn't just a midfield player or a striker or a forward, he was simply a 'footballer', full stop.

When you consider that David Platt was subsequently sold by us to Bari, of which more later, for £5.5m, that extra £50,000, which you could say was actually provided by Rangers when they paid the extra on Mark Walters, was small change, indeed. You will also see what I mean when I say that Graham Taylor performed a magnificent team-building job for Aston Villa FC in that the fee when Platt was sold was to underwrite Ron Atkinson's signings in 1991-92.

Likewise, those critics who, over the years, have written that 'Doug Ellis won't cough up the transfer money' don't know the half. No-one has heard any of the club's ex-managers make such a claim.

Actually, there has been one, though it was said tongue in cheek. I read in a newspaper that shares Tommy Docherty had purchased in Aston Villa for a few pounds in 1968 had gone up in value to £25,000 as a result of the 1997 flotation, and that this, the Doc said, was 'more than Doug Ellis ever gave me to buy new players'.

Another of his witty one-liners. All I can say in reply is that, if it were true, which it wasn't, then when he told me that he had paid Luton Town £100,000 for Bruce Rioch and his brother, Neil, all those years ago he must have done OK with the £75,000 'surplus'. My turn for a wise-crack now, Doc...

However, the signing of Platt was to prove a master-stroke as he scored five goals in the final eleven Second Division fixtures, leading up to the tense 0-0 draw at Swindon which took us into second place and promotion by a heart-beat.

In my mind's eye I can still see Graham's face down in the dressing room area at the County Ground and also recall the warm embrace that signalled our mutual mixed feelings of relief, triumph and respect.

Back in the First Division in 1988-89, that first season predictably proved to be hard work as we struggled to a precarious 17th position and Platt began to make a name for himself.

It was during a summer tour before the next season that another signing took place under Graham's reign that could ultimately prove to be even more inspired than that of Platt.

We were in the West Indies playing in Trinidad & Tobago against the island team in a stadium without stands. Graham and I were side-by-side on a bench beside what was little better than a parks pitch and I remember after about ten minutes into the game nudging Graham and saying: "Eh, what do you think about this boy up front?" Graham said: "I like him." We didn't even know his name but I was excited enough about what I saw to go to the other bench twenty yards away where the manager of the national side was sitting with his coaches.

He told me that the player in question was named Dwight Yorke. I asked him if the lad had any honours and he told me he had seventeen caps. I asked his age and was told 'sixteen' (though it transpired that he was seventeen).

I said "You mean under-18 caps". He said "no". I said "you mean under-21 caps". He said "no". He meant full caps. I couldn't believe it. Seventeen full caps at 16, as we understood at that time.

All this convinced me that I should suggest to Graham that we invite this young Dwight Yorke over, with his local club manager in Tobago, to Villa Park with a view to signing him. Shortly after our return home we sent three air tickets and Dwight travelled to Villa Park with his manager and his aunt, a very attractive lady barrister, who acted for him and his club. His club were delighted to accept a sum of £10,000 for a 17-year-old unknown and Dwight's aunt was equally delighted to advise Dwight to accept the contract we offered. The transaction was amicably settled in our boardroom. We were confident we had done a good deal, though we probably couldn't have predicted that, seven years later, we wouldn't sell him for a thousand times that figure.

Looking back I feel that Graham and I forged a sound working relationship and, certainly, we have remained friends. We all have our qualities and shortcomings and, to me, Graham sometimes seemed a little precious. He liked to be loved, admired, praised and never took kindly to criticism. I suspected he was jealous of the high-profile I have always had myself and would have preferred a chairman with no public profile at all.

Strange that, really. I never did wear funny spectacles and shiny suits while playing the piano and singing to millions of people all over the world, like his previous chairman with whom he has been re-united at Watford FC.

The average football fan never gets to hear of many of the negotiating situations that evolve behind the scenes in any football club. There was, for instance, the sale by Graham Taylor of the Scottish international striker Alan McInally to Bayern Munich in 1989 for £1.2m.

An important feature of the arrangement was that the German club, with whom we had links dating back to when we beat them in the European Cup Final of 1982, would play a friendly game at Villa Park for which we would retain the proceeds as part of the fee, less their expenses.

To this day that agreement has never been honoured. Whenever we have contacted them on the subject, which has been frequently over the years, they have never had an available date that was convenient to themselves.

On more than one occasion I have raised the issue with 'The Kaiser' himself, Franz Beckenbauer. This included the time when I found myself, at the England-Germany semi-final of the European Championships at Wembley in the summer of 1996, with Beckenbauer next to me on my left and Pele on my right.

Strange, really, the sort of stunts that life can pull on you. As a lad I would probably have dreamed of being between two of the world's greatest-ever footballers, though we would have been out on the pitch wearing football boots not sitting in the stand in suits.

However, I took the opportunity to ask Beckenbauer when Bayern

Munich were coming to Villa Park to honour that agreement. I'm still waiting for the answer.

It reminded me of the time, I believe it was after Graham Taylor had left, that I made an attempt to offer Franz the job of manager of Aston Villa.

He has a house just outside Kitzbühel in Austria and, by chance, we sometimes both went skiing at the nearby resort. We had also spent some time together when, with our wives, we once had a meal in the McGregor Suite at Villa Park. Heidi is German, remember, while Franz speaks fluent English.

Consequently I felt I knew them, as a couple, when I attempted to speak to him to establish if he would be interested in joining Aston Villa.

Having rung his number a lady answered the telephone and I chatted to her for a moment or two on the basis that, as she would no doubt recall, we had dined together in our foursome and had also met at the ski resort. After a while she broke in and said: "I'm sorry, I think you must have the wrong wife..." How was I to know that, in the interim, he had changed partners? However, I passed on the message that he could ring me if he were interested in being Aston Villa's manager, but he never did take up the option. That, of course, could depend on whether 'the wrong wife' ever passed on my message. One interesting conversation I do recall holding with him, when he was a player, was on the question of the excessive number of matches clubs sometimes play. When I said that we had played fifty-five he shrugged and said "So what? We play seventy-five".

I said that I couldn't believe that figure because the German Bundesliga was smaller than our then First Division with only 18 clubs.

His reply was that every week they flew somewhere or other around the world to play a cash-raising, prestige friendly game "otherwise we don't earn our money.

"We play in Hong Kong one week, maybe South America soon after, with league games in between", he said. He also reckoned that they had asked their coach for an increase in terms and had been told "Fine. We'll play another five friendlies each year to pay for it..."

I don't think I dare try that approach the next time one of our player's contract comes up for renewal.

However, to return to the Graham Taylor era, he proved his merit as a team-builder, planner and motivator by steering us into that runners-up place in the 1989-90 season when David Platt scored 19 goals in 37 First Division games and earned his place in Bobby Robson's World Cup squad.

When taking an over-view of Graham Taylor's contribution to the club the obvious conclusions would be that David Platt and Dwight Yorke were his pre-eminent captures. There would be, however, an unforgivable omission. Let us never forget one other signing which rates among Aston Villa's, and certainly Graham's, best ever.

The decision to enlist Paul McGrath from an unhappy situation in which he found himself at Old Trafford, in August 1989, was in my view as enlightened as any managerial move in my memory.

Macca, as he became known, was simply a joy to watch on the field of play and a delightful person to have around the club. His personal problems have been well-documented already and I don't propose to rake over them, other than to say that there were times of potential trouble when he seemed to regard me as a father figure and it was a role I was more than happy to play.

One problem any memoir-writer must encounter when outlining successes, as compared to being self-deprecatory about failures, is that it can come across as a case of glory-seeking. Thus, rather than use my own description of Paul's experiences at Villa Park I reproduce here an extract from his own life story: *Ooh Aah Paul McGrath* (Mainstream Publishing). In a passage concerning his move to Aston Villa he wrote: "I couldn't help but be impressed when I first sat down to talk serious business (with Aston Villa)... there were no agents involved. Just me, my wife, Graham and his chairman, Doug Ellis. They laid it on the line. They wanted me to be part of the new Aston Villa. They wanted to build a team that would challenge for the title. They felt I was cheap at £450,000 from a United only too willing to get rid of me at any price... To this day I do not believe there is a crooked bone in Aston Villa. The manager and chairman were first-class."

Could there be a better testimonial than this, from a more popular and talented footballer, to endorse my favourite principle of players, manager and chairman working together for the benefit of any club?

Here Graham sensibly accepted the merit of the principle along with an experienced, world-class player and Aston Villa went on to enjoy seven wonderful years of Paul McGrath's services.

Ironically, by proving for the first time that he could operate successfully as the manager of a major club, as distinct from leading a smaller one from obscurity, he became the Football Association's choice as the man to replace Robson.

How We Nearly Lost David Platt

The approach duly came to me from the FA and the then president Bert Millichip, a long-time associate of mine through his original status as chairman of West Bromwich Albion even before his elevation to the figurehead at Lancaster Gate.

Naturally, we didn't want to lose our manager at such a crucial time but, obviously, being offered the job of managing your country is a very exceptional case. There was no special clause in Graham's contract to meet this eventuality but what were we to do? When Graham came to me and told me that he wished to accept the appointment because it was what he had wanted since he was about nine-years-of-age, it was a case of Hobson's Choice.

Well, almost. Graham had about two years of his contract to run, a contract which he had undertaken with a total commitment to Aston Villa Football Club. Fours years earlier, remember, when given permission by Manchester City to approach Billy McNeill, the understanding was that Villa would 'buy up' his contract in full if he were to join us, which we did.

The feelings of the Villa board as a whole therefore were that if Graham were to leave us managerless after leading us to the runners-up place, then the Football Association would have to pay up his contract as we had done with Manchester City.

Once that principle had been accepted and established the negotiations were between Bert Millichip and myself and they came to a head when we met at the Football Association's summer conference.

We had asked for the full salary value of the unexpired period of the contract, which was around £250,000, to be paid to Aston Villa. The FA wanted to pay £200,000, hence that eventual get-together of Bert and I at the summer conference.

Bert took me aside and said "Look Doug, let's settle at £225,000" an offer which I accepted and duly said "goodbye" to Manager number seven.

Chapter Twelve

"Sack Me" Invited Gentleman Jo

The loss of Graham Taylor, who went off to vainly attempt to help England qualify for the 1994 World Cup in the USA left Villa, yet again, to seek a new manager. We quickly discovered if we didn't already suspect it, that there were not too many around.

I did, however, come up with one intriguing personality, not a familiar one in this country outside of those who follow the European game closely, but someone whom I met during the World Cup in Italy.

History now confirms that it was Dr Jozef Venglos, a hugely respected national team coach from the former Czechoslovakia, now split into the Czech Republic and Slovakia. Jo was one of the most respected coaches in the Eastern bloc, a highly-intelligent man and fine former Slovan Bratislava player who spoke fluent English along with six other languages and was a PhD graduate from Bratislava University. As manager of the club for whom he played with distinction he won two Czech Championships and also helped lead his country, as assistant coach, in becoming European Champions in 1976.

Later as Czech national coach he led them to third place in the 1980 European Championships and to the World Cup Finals in Spain in 1982.

Also he had held coaching appointments all around the world and was an official adviser to FIFA and also one of their coaching instructors. With this wealth of knowledge and expertise I felt he could bring a new perspective to the English game because of his grasp of continental coaching methods. Bear in mind, despite reaching the semi-final of the

World Cup that year, our players were widely regarded as being well behind the best of the foreigners. Perhaps coaches like Jo Venglos could help us to improve on that reputation? This was our theory, anyway, when we introduced him to a Villa Park press conference on a Saturday in July 1990. I have been teased since about having kicked off by saying "This man needs no introduction" to local press guys who hadn't the faintest idea who he was! They soon found out when we distributed his lengthy CV.

Jo actually took up his duties in earnest in August and his arrival at our Bodymoor Heath training ground coincided with a temperature of about 105 degrees Fahrenheit, the hottest English day since records began.

Jo was a lovely man, gentle, respectful, sincere and anxious to prove himself to the English, whom he clearly held in very high esteem.

Despite the unbearable heatwave the 51-year-old dived into a practice game, dashing around in the sweltering heat like a teenager, giving and accepting passes, making tackles, the lot. By now there were batteries of local and national media with TV cameras, microphones and the usual paraphernalia.

Another press conference was set up in our gym, which was several degrees hotter and even more humid than it had been outside. They all wanted to show him, in his sweat-soaked training gear and were puzzled as to why they had to wait a considerable time for his appearance into the TV arc lights.

When he arrived Jo, bless his heart, was dressed in a suit and tie, but with beads of perspiration streaming down his face, determined not to let the club down by appearing in his role as manager 'improperly dressed'. He was correct and proper at all times and, in that regard alone, set an example to everyone. He was accustomed to working on the Continent where coaches are mainly just that, employees who carry out the club's policies, unlike in this country where the manager expects to be, and often is, all-powerful.

Jo had never before enjoyed the kind of status he had at Villa Park but he could not come to terms with the sums of money that were being paid for signing new players in this country, a fact which probably explains why he did not strengthen the team as it needed in order to build on Graham Taylor's foundations. He did sign Gary Penrice from Bristol Rovers though the player he really liked at that time was Vinny Samways.

It was a great shame that his reign at Villa Park did not work out as we would have liked. The players were gob-smacked by some of his modern methods of preparation, by his knowledge of all aspects of an athlete's requirements and by his courteous manner.

They were taught warming up and warming down procedures they had never encountered before with different stretching exercises for all the various muscles, all things that have now become more common in our games but were very half-hearted at that time.

In retrospect I'm not sure that some of the English club managers were too happy about his being here and taking, as they perhaps thought, one of 'their' top jobs. I sometimes had cause to wonder.

He remained a very modest man who resided whilst he was here in one of the club's houses along with his charming wife and two sons, one of whom is a barrister.

The bottom line, however sad to recall, was that it didn't work out, for whatever reason. By the end of December we had won but four of our opening nineteen First Division games. I do recall appointing Peter Withe as his assistant to introduce some English-style communication and we just about avoided losing the First Division status we cherished so much, in 17th place.

Give Jozef Venglos his due, as I always would, he was so honest in his self-assessment that he came to me about a month before the end of the season to say that if I was dissatisfied with his efforts then he would stand down voluntarily. That was something new I can assure you, having a manager questioning whether he was earning his keep.

I recall him saying: "I love it here and you have always been very good to me but if you feel, for the sake of the club, that you ought to appoint someone else, it will not be a problem." Although he had signed a two-year contract there was a 'break' clause in it to the effect that he would leave before the end of the term subject to proper compensation being paid. This was the arrangement we implemented, most amicably, at the end of one season in the mutual knowledge that an idea that seemed a perfectly good one when undertaken had not been successful.

There was no animosity whatsoever. In fact we have been in touch from time to time and, when we played Slovan Bratislava in the UEFA Cup of September 1994, Jo was there waiting for us and visibly delighted to renew acquaintances. It was an education to walk around the beautiful city of Prague with him, as I did on one occasion in company with our secretary Steve Stride, he was such a popular person. They simply idolise him. Wherever we walked, at whatever time of the day, there would be people of all ages recognising him and wanting to shake his hand, sometimes crossing the thoroughfare to do so. In return he had that wonderful capacity and willingness to respond courteously and give a little of his time to chat to them.

I was with him when he signed autographs for about ten minutes, outside a restaurant, after midnight, while being careful not to leave anyone out.

Without commission or compensation he still advises us on players in his region whom he feels might be successful at Aston Villa. His relationship with the club was never less than totally cordial, but I can state categorically and with total honesty that I have been able to settle satisfactorily, on the very day of departure, with every dismissed manager except one, and they have gone away with a suitable cheque in their pocket.

And so the hunt was on for a replacement for Jo Venglos. This time, however, I did not have to look very far. Waiting in the wings was a certain former Aston Villa player who still lived in the Midlands and who had always wanted to manage Aston Villa Football Club.

Chapter Thirteen

Life With Big Ron

Once Jozef Venglos had left Villa Park it proved easier than we expected to appoint a successor in July 1991. Just as Graham Taylor had made himself available four years earlier so, this time, it was Ron Atkinson who tossed his hat into the ring virtually from Day One. Ron had led Sheffield Wednesday from relegation the season before, straight back into the First Division. Only a matter of weeks earlier his leadership had taken what was then the Rumbelows Football League Cup to Hillsborough.

Reflecting on his situation as it must have been at that time one could imagine his psychological dilemma. Although born in Liverpool he was brought up in Birmingham, as a Villa supporter who achieved his young dream of being signed by the club as an apprentice.

Once his playing days were over his ambition was to be manager of Aston Villa and, four years earlier, had been a 'possible' until Graham Taylor made it known that he was available.

Now the job was vacant just at a time when he was established as a folk-hero at Hillsborough. What should he do? Presumably the temptation was too strong to resist. He telephoned our then secretary, now director-secretary Steve Stride, to make it known that he was interested in joining Villa if we were interested in discussing the possibility.

Yes, indeed we were, but first he would have to sort out his own situation at Sheffield Wednesday. That wouldn't be easy for obvious reasons and Ron was presumably left with deeply mixed emotions and a great deal of soul-searching. One part of the equation, and very much in our favour quite apart from his ambition to manage Aston Villa was that, while he wanted to continue to live in the Midlands, he was genuinely tired of commuting each day from his home near Birmingham to Sheffield.

Jo Venglos left 'by mutual consent' on May 29th and the usual media guessing game began. One interesting name included in the speculation proved later to have been inspired crystal-ball gazing, namely Brian Little. Others were Kenny Dalglish, who had left Liverpool but not yet joined Blackburn Rovers, Bruce Rioch and Arthur Cox. At that stage no-one so much as suggested Ron Atkinson, simply because he was being offered a new two-year contract by the Sheffield Wednesday chairman, David Richards. Within a couple of days, however, Ron resigned from Hillsborough and, as a result of his phone call to Steve Stride, we were able to confidently announce his readiness to join Villa. It all seemed straightforward enough at the time. In reality his appointment proved to be anything but that.

Ron went back to Sheffield to attend an end-of-the-season celebration of the club's dual success and being back in that environment and meeting up with his chairman prompted a change of heart. I received a telephone call from him on around June 1st to say that he was staying at Hillsborough after all, a decision I felt I had to reluctantly accept.

Thus, our search was on again and this time the name of Joe Royle appeared in newspapers as the new favourite. Alongside the renewed speculation Atkinson was being quoted as saying that, when he walked into his Hillsborough office and sat down, he realised he would be 'barmy' to think of leaving. We understood that. But we also knew that he would regard himself as 'barmy' if he turned down the Villa job, the very one he had always wanted. In this lingering air of uncertainty all was quiet for about a week as the headlines gradually subsided.

Unknown possibly to Ron, since the well-being of Aston Villa was as imperative to us as his relationship with Sheffield Wednesday was to him, we had by now another name available as Plan B if Plan A broke down.

That name must remain secret to avoid any embarrassment, but I do recall Steve Stride coming to me to say: "Chairman, we have either got to appoint Ron Atkinson this week or reject the idea and go for our second choice.

"Why don't we sort it out by going and knocking on Ron's door?" I could hardly argue with such logic so this is what we did. Steve and I sat and talked to Ron and his charming wife Maggie at their home for at least an hour and when we left he had accepted the job and an excellent contractual deal which he had firmly negotiated for himself.

I was delighted to have him, no argument about that because one could only admire the fact that he had won the FA Cup twice with Manchester United and had more recently won promotion and the League Cup for Sheffield Wednesday.

Much earlier in his career it had not escaped my notice that he had learned the managerial ropes successfully with non-League Kettering Town before taking Cambridge United to promotion from the Fourth Division to the Second Division in successive seasons. He had also led West Bromwich Albion to an FA Cup semi-final and into the UEFA Cup, sharing in the development of Bryan Robson, before moving to Old Trafford. Even over and above all this, one admired the kind of entertaining attacking football his teams always played, his relationship with the media, and the attention he attracted to his club with his TV personality.

My first contacts with Ron, years before, were in his Kettering Town days when I was still running my MATO package-deal trips to Spain and elsewhere. I used to make it known to the Professional Footballers' Association that free flights were available to their members during the month of May, subject to availability. This was a facility I could offer to fill empty seats on any of my twenty-seven weekly flights to various locations. Ron would ring me, remind me that he was an ex-Aston Villa player, and would take advantage of the offer.

Later, after he joined West Bromwich Albion we had quite a deal of social contact at, for instance, the old regular monthly luncheons staged by the Midland Soccer Writers. I used to pull his leg that his brother Graham, a very nice, quiet chap who played with him at Oxford United, was a better player than him. I liked Graham and Ron's late father, Fred, an ex-wartime Royal Navy man like myself. Consequently Ron and I knew each other quite well when he became our manager just at the time when the club needed someone with his experience, expertise and crowd-pulling charisma.

Big Ron's appointment put Aston Villa firmly in the national limelight, no doubt about that. TV cameras, still cameras, microphones, football writers packed into our North Stand banqueting suite as never before for the press conference to confirm his arrival.

I well remember sitting with him in my office waiting to meet the media.

Our mood was one of cheerful celebration and optimism. He sank a brandy or two while we were waiting to go into the press conference. Once there he was his usual wisecracking self 'on stage' and the whole buoyant feeling was that exciting times were ahead.

I seem to recall a moment when I interrupted something he was saying and Ron responded by saying: "See, he's interfering already..." to big laughs all round from the assembled media. In retrospect I sense that there was a barely-concealed message in that comment.

From the point of view of available transfer resources the timing was spot-on. His arrival more or less coincided with the Italian club Bari making repeated bids for David Platt who, a year earlier, had become a World star along with Paul Gascoigne because of their displays for England in Italia 90. We had rejected two Bari approaches at £5.5m before Ron was appointed, but the situation was still boiling up when he joined us. Life can and does continually throw up some unpredictable situations and this was one of them. During his Manchester United days, with a playing staff packed with good players at all levels, Ron had released a young Platt on a free transfer to Crewe Alexandra. Now, some six years later, he was taking over at Villa Park just as Platt was leaving having, in the meantime, become one of the most expensive players in the world. I seem to recall reading somewhere a classic comment from Ron that he had had David Platt on his books at two different clubs and had never so much as picked him for his first team.

There were delays in the Platt transfer for several reasons. David was on an England tour of Australia and Malaysia, Ron had some summer holiday organised and I was abroad for a while myself. Eventually, on Thursday July 18th, the Bari president and owner Vincenzo Mattarese came to Birmingham and met Ron Atkinson and Platt, while I was out of the country.

The name 'Mattarese' is big, powerful and influential in Italy. Vincenzo has a huge business in the construction industry and is said to have supplied the cement for half of the nation's motorways, a fact that was later to inspire one of Big Ron's classic wisecracks. One of Vincenzo's brothers was a cardinal in the Vatican and another, Antonio, was president of the Italian Football Federation. They are the sort of family who tend to get their way.

After this visit the player was satisfied with the terms offered, but Ron, give him his due, was asking for £6m, about £1.5m more than Bari's original offer. At that meeting an appointment was made for Bari representatives to come back to Birmingham on the Saturday morning to meet me at Villa Park. We'd had previous dealings with the ambitious club from the south of Italy some years before when we sold them Gordon Cowans and Paul Rideout. One slightly unusual feature of our dealings this time was that David Platt's representative was Tony Stephens who had learned the ropes as Aston Villa's own commercial manager.

Tony had helped Platt to a magnificent contract which was reported in the press as being worth some £4m over three years. The whole story was all very big news, indeed, because it was a record deal and the forerunner of others that were to follow as fees escalated each season.

I recall looking out of my Villa Park office window on that July Saturday morning onto a scene teeming with a large press entourage from both countries. I gather they had been at Birmingham airport to meet the Italians coming in and the scene had now shifted to our car park. When you deal with the Italians on footballing matters everything seems a shade larger than life.

By now I had received a fax message from Bari with a written offer of £5.5m, a compromise between their first offers and Ron Atkinson's demand. Signor Mattarese was not on this trip, having already done the spadework. His big, impressive general manager, Franco Janich, was his representative with the authority to complete a deal. Mattarese's club vice-president and a commercial director were with Signor Janich, ready and authorised to set a new UK transfer record.

After lengthy discussions, with the media circus still camped outside, I sensed that £5.5m was their final offer, which I accepted, while carefully imposing one condition, namely that Aston Villa would be entitled to fifty per cent of any profit from a subsequent sell-on. Such a future deal was a distinct possibility since Juventus had made it known already that they admired Platt's work in Italia 90 and his progress with Aston Villa ever since. The sale of Platt and also of Tony Cascarino to Glasgow Rangers gave Ron considerable resources with which to fund the building of his own team.

Once that first season got underway fate stage-managed another ironical situation when Ron Atkinson's first match as manager of Aston Villa was away to, of all clubs, Sheffield Wednesday, whom he had left amid so much acrimony. Trevor Francis was now their manager, on Big Ron's recommendation.

Such was the ill-feeling on the part of the minority idiot fringe that can give every club a bad name, there was talk of death threats and of Ron needing a police escort. None of this seemed to bother him one jot and, moreover, he strode through it all untroubled before leaving with a satisfying record of played one, won one.

Atkinson's early signings included such players as Dalian Atkinson, Kevin Richardson, Steve Staunton, Shaun Teale, Garry Parker, Cyrille Regis, Earl Barrett and others in completely rebuilding his squad. Some of these acquisitions reflected the undoubted managerial skills for which we had appointed him. Kevin Richardson was seen, rightly it transpired, as a player who could help Villa to honours just as he had done with both Everton and Arsenal, whom he had assisted to the Championship. He was Ron's skipper and a very dedicated one, too.

Shaun Teale was an unsung player with Bournemouth when Ron signed him for a mere £300,000 fee and the player became one of the most effective defenders in the First Division. Steve Staunton, a very shrewd capture from Liverpool, has given Aston Villa superb service and Liverpool, I'm sure, regard him as one of their worst sales.

In that first season, with his restructured squad, Ron Atkinson took the club ten places up the old First Division from Jo Venglos's 17th and also reached a sixth-round FA Cup-tie at Liverpool.

A good team was taking shape and the quality of the passing football was also an encouraging sign. It would be nice to reflect that everything was going according to plan yet, the truth was, that it did not take long for me to realise that the kind of chairman-manager relationship I have referred to earlier, and would have liked to have had with him, was not going to evolve. He did his job and I did mine but often we were, let's say 'distant'.

Ron remained just a big boy at heart, in my observations, and I suspect he would not have argued had you referred to him as a frustrated player sitting in the manager's chair as the best alternative to being 'one of the lads'. In his wisecracking way he used to refer to himself sometimes as 'the player-manager'.

Never a day went by without his being out at Bodymoor Heath, playing in a six-a-side seeing himself as either Pele, or Cruyff or Matthews or whatever legendary name took his fancy.

The fans loved this Jack-The-Lad image and the players responded well to his imposing presence among them. I had no argument against all this.

Indeed, one of the qualities that attracted me to him as a potential manager was that he was very much a 'player's manager'.

From my perspective, however, cracks soon appeared in his image. Being at the training ground playing football every morning was fine up to a point. What I found hard to accept was that, although he had an office at Villa Park, we never saw him, even after training was completed, unless he had a very specific reason to meet someone there. It was as though, for the most part, he saw his job as beginning and ending at the training ground.

When he accepted the appointment it was agreed that he could continue TV work as long as it did not interfere with his Aston Villa duties.

Naively, I guess, I imagined that he would inform me when he was undertaking such work. Not so, I'm afraid.

There was a classic example, early in 1993, of how this lack of contact between us seriously affected the running of the club and the possible loss of an important signing at the right price. The player in question was Andy Cole when he was at Bristol City. I knew Ron Atkinson fancied him because he had told me as much in one of our discussions.

When I was at the FA offices at Lancaster Gate one day, for a meeting, I was in the foyer, as we were about to leave, chatting to the then Bristol City chairman, Leslie Kew. He said to me: "Are you still interested in Cole?" My reply was: "Yes, if our manager is still interested and if the price is right." The fee previously quoted for Cole had been prohibitive, bearing in mind that he had not then been fully tried out at the highest level. If my memory serves me correctly they had been asking in excess of £2m.

"Newcastle and Liverpool are both messing us around," said Leslie. "If you are serious about wanting him you can shake my hand at £1.2m." It seemed an excellent deal to me, knowing of Ron's interest, so I shook his hand on the condition that it was subject to the manager's approval and confirmation.

Leslie Kew accepted the principle and, though he had a train to catch, was prepared to wait while I telephoned Ron there and then from the FA offices, hopefully to set up the deal. I recall that it was approximately one o'clock lunchtime, a time in the day when you would expect to be able to track your manager down somewhere or other.

However, for the next half-an-hour I made telephone calls, to the training ground, to Villa Park, his home, his mobile number, all to no avail. No-one seemed to know where he was.

Eventually, Mr Kew pointed out that he was in danger of missing his train back to Bristol and would have to go. As he left I promised to call him at his home as and when I was able to speak to my manager. I never made that telephone call to Leslie Kew. To this day I don't know where Ron was. The nearest I got to finding out were suggestions from some people to whom I spoke that he was 'abroad'.

The outcome of that sorry situation was that Andy Cole signed for Newcastle United in March 1993 for a reported £1.75m and was very successful at St James's Park before his £7m move to Manchester United just under two years later.

I would sometimes see Atkinson's face on telly, or hear his voice, from various places in this country and abroad when I had no idea that this was where our manager happened to be.

If I wanted to talk club business with him I had to ring him at the training ground or at his home. Even the courtesy of an occasional visit to my office for a chat would have been better than these periodic phone calls.

Talking of offices, one of the early breaches in my respect for his managerial style came over a match-day office we had specially prepared for him. It was in the building that was originally the Lions club and later the club shop and Promotions offices.

A Players' Lounge was created there with a manager's office next door to it, strategically-placed I would have thought for obvious reasons of supervision.

Ron looked at the office and said he didn't want it. Instead he plumped for another room, well away from the Players' Lounge and right next door to the Directors' private guest room. It was intended for apprentices and reserves on match days to save them hanging around the corridor, but was taken over by the manager.

The walls were very thin and not sound-proofed and Ron and his match-day guests, including usually the opposition manager, tended to get a little noisy when they were winding down with a drink after games.

Sometimes the raucous hilarity echoed around the Directors room to everyone's embarrassment. No-one minds a laugh and a joke, especially when the day's job is done, but it wasn't the most discreet of signals for the manager to send out if his team had lost and possibly played badly.

I well recall one visiting chairman saying to me: "You're not the Doug Ellis I know if you are prepared to put up with that sort of behaviour..." And, talking about his team, they were well away from him with their own guests drinking at the club's expense, often for a couple of hours after a match.

Some of those guests bordered on being rated as undesirables who did not conduct themselves too well, especially after several free drinks. More than once they caused embarrassment to security men who were rightly trying to close the club for the night.

It seemed to me that if the manager had accepted the office which had been sensibly planned for him his very presence nearby would have prevented some of those excesses. The manager does, after all, have a free hand in terms of the players' code of conduct, and their discipline.

Another factor, incidentally, that truly does annoy me is when things are reported in the press about the club, and players in particular, that I know nothing about. I always expect managers, and other executives at the club to keep me fully informed each day about what is going on. There are few things more embarrassing than being stopped, sometimes by an ordinary supporter in the street, and asked about matters which have appeared in the press and, as chairman, I know nothing about them. To be fair all but one of my managers have understood this request and complied with it by keeping me informed to the best of their ability.

Chapter Fourteen

Atkinson's Downfall

Ron Atkinson's second season coincided with the start of the Premier League, the Sky TV money and all the revolution in football finance that the advances entailed.

Ray Houghton had joined Steve Staunton as an Irish Republic international import from Liverpool, but Cyrille Regis had been a short-term stop-gap as main striker and needed replacing. Another inquiry at Anfield was Ron's answer, this time for Dean Saunders. The Welsh international had scored 23 goals for Liverpool since moving from Derby County including a record number in European goals yet, strangely, he was not unanimously regarded as a success there.

A club record figure of around £2.5m was being discussed for the Welsh international, manager to manager, around August-September, but I'm afraid more strain was placed on our relationship when I became convinced that a better deal could be achieved for Aston Villa FC. As a result I made some overtures myself before the negotiations were successfully concluded for £2.3m.

As a result of my intervention we had, indeed, secured an improved agreement but it meant a delay of a week or two while Liverpool and the player pondered our bid. This caused speculation in the press about the chairman interfering with the manager's transfer policy. I heard subsequently that the usual group of local football writers who assembled each Friday in Ron's office at Bodymoor Heath got the impression that the deal was almost clinched on that particular day and they waited outside for further news. Apparently it was at this time that I informed the manager that I was to talk to Liverpool myself. The press were able to glean from his subsequent demeanour, allied to the fact that the deal was not clinched after all, that there was friction between us.

Speculation about all this in the papers led to my having a chat with him along the lines that he should be putting out the message that we were all pulling together for the benefit of the club.

The reality was that we had not started that season especially well and the last thing we needed was reports of internal unrest. Early home attendances were below 20,000, only one of our opening six matches had been won and this sequence included two draws and a defeat out of three at home. By now the team contained some seven players whom Ron had signed himself. As a result of my chat with him on the question of relieving public fears about our working relationship he was persuaded to go out onto the pitch with the microphone before the kick-off against Crystal Palace on September 5th to assure the crowd that the Dean Saunders signing would be completed shortly and that everyone at the club was pulling in the same direction. But were we...? The game was won 3-0 and Saunders arrived in time for the next match, against Leeds United at Elland Road. By this time Ron Atkinson's transfer account balanced out about even, with £20m-worth of sales and a similar amount spent on players. No complaints about that at all, and the arrival of Dean Saunders gave everyone a boost.

A 1-1 draw at Leeds preceded Saunders' home debut, against his former club Liverpool, when nearly 38,000 fans flocked in and Deano scored twice in a memorable 4-2 win. Dalian Atkinson also scored and the pair became a popular strike pair with the public, who now had high hopes that the team they called 'Big Fat Ron's Claret-and-Blue Army' was on its way to big things.

It proved to be an outstanding season with a challenge being made to become the very first Premiership Champions. This wasn't to be, but we did finish runners-up behind Manchester United without further signings being made, no further noticeable friction between the manager and myself and all the signs looking good.

Season 1993-94, with our magnificent Coca Cola Cup victory over Manchester United following on to runners-up place in the Premiership the previous season was basically an encouraging period for everyone concerned. Our long-term aim to be challenging for honours and a place in Europe each season, a reasonable objective I have always maintained for a club of Aston Villa's stature and volume and loyalty of our support, seemed to be on track.

Playing progress was there to be seen. Ron had skilfully nurtured two superb young players in goalkeeper Mark Bosnich and defender Ugo Ehiogu, while Andy Townsend had been signed from Chelsea for £2.1m. The fee, we conceded, was a touch high for a 30-year-old but the manager said he would be good value, and he was to be proved absolutely right. We had also signed striker Guy Whittingham from Portsmouth for £1.1m.

A UEFA Cup place had been secured and though we were dismissed in the second round by Deportivo La Coruna, the Spaniards proved themselves to be one of the strongest teams in Europe at that time.

It was in the Coca Cola sponsored Football League Cup that Ron Atkinson's team shone. Even when left 1-3 down to Tranmere Rovers in the first leg of the semi-final at Prenton Park, a club with such nostalgic connections for myself, we came back to reach Wembley after equalising almost on the 90 minutes and going on to win the penalty shoot-out in thrilling fashion.

The atmosphere of the refurbished and modernised Villa Park that memorable night was absolutely electric, the supporters were right behind the club and Ron Atkinson was confirming the managerial skills he had illustrated previously elsewhere.

If that was exciting and rewarding, the Final was an even more momentous occasion as Alex Ferguson's Manchester United were totally outwitted and outplayed. Atkinson demonstrably loves the cup competitions and taking centre stage at Wembley where his personality, experience and self-confidence were of great benefit to the team in terms of leadership.

To keep things relaxed he had his personal friend, Stan Boardman, the scouser comic, on the team coach on the way to the stadium, and in the dressing room, keeping the lads amused and Wembley nerves at bay. Stan was at our banquet afterwards also and Big Ron himself, was up on stage with his rendering of 'New York, New York', which he changed to 'Dwight Yorke, Dwight Yorke'. It was a terrific atmosphere with excellent input from our manager who, during his career, had now won the FA Cup twice for Manchester United, the League Cup for Sheffield Wednesday, by beating his former club and had repeated the dose for Aston Villa.

No-one admired his achievements more than I did and no-one wanted more than I did to see him build on the foundations which he had put down. Sadly, however, this proved to be the peak of Ron Atkinson's success at Villa Park, not the start of a plateau of achievement, and the downslope was unexpectedly steep. By the end of the season when we had drifted to tenth place in the Premiership with only three League wins in fourteen matches since the Coca Cola Cup semi-final at the end of February, there were very clear danger signals.

We had several players, albeit quality ones, who were around the thirty mark and over. I don't profess to be a football manager but anyone who has watched the game over a lengthy period of time gets a gut feeling about certain things. Mine was that we needed to strengthen our squad with some top-class, younger players, during the summer. In short, fresh legs were essential.

There was absolutely no doubt in my mind that a high proportion of our supporters felt the same, even though Big Ron had become something of a cult figure by then. Imagine my surprise then, when in chatting to him, I discovered that he was firmly convinced that his squad, as it was, would be Premiership top-six material for 1994-95, without any additions.

Frankly, I disagreed with him and wasn't convinced that his best place for a portion of that summer was in the USA covering the World Cup for TV. We're always told by those managers who want to see the World Cup that it is an essential part of their football education but I saw no evidence of Villa benefiting from Ron's USA trip.

I do recall, while he was there, that the Manchester United chairman, Martin Edwards, told me that Dion Dublin was available for transfer. That, I felt, could be valuable information.

The general feeling among Villa folk was that while Dean Saunders and Dalian Atkinson had obvious strengths in attack we lacked what might be termed an orthodox 'centre forward' type.

By way of passing on this information to Atkinson I telephoned him in the United States but it seemed he was having a meal at the time and was most reluctant to speak to me. If my memory serves me correctly he indicated that 'he did not fancy' Dublin, so that was the end of that.

In the event the only signings that close season when Ron returned from the World Cup in the immediate run up to the season, were Ghanaian Nii Lamptey on loan from Anderlecht and Phil King from Sheffield Wednesday before John Fashanu was signed for £1.35m from Wimbledon, aged 31.

Another mature pair of legs. Also, of course, Fashanu had extensive business interests, apart from having to record instalments of *The Gladiators* TV programme and was some sort of travelling ambassador for UNICEF. Because of these commitments he did not have to train or play if he did not wish to.

In fact, he played only thirteen games, scoring three goals for us before his playing career came to an end. Early in the season he was out with Achilles tendon trouble and then, at Old Trafford in February, he was stretchered off after a challenge with Ryan Giggs with what proved to be serious cruciate ligament damage.

Soon it was clear that he would not be able to continue playing, so we naturally took the necessary steps to implement the appropriate insurance policy covering the cost of his transfer.

This necessitated written expert opinions from two specialists that his injury made it impossible for him to play on in League football. One of these specialists, based in the south-west, was one he selected himself.

Both of these medical reports stated that he was unfit to continue playing professional football because the knee damage could not be put right by surgery.

Here I have to concede that I found John Fashanu's IQ to be as high as any player with whom I have ever had dealings. His ability to negotiate articulately was unsurpassed in my experience.

When we put it to him that his career was over, and that we were to claim the insurance cover he replied that unless he received fifty per cent of that cover he would continue to visit specialists for further opinions because, in his view he could get himself fit again. He would work hard on his knee until, eventually, he would be able to play again.

The next two specialists he visited, he told us, would be in France and Canada respectively. Meanwhile, he would remain on our books, we would pay him his wages, and our medical and recuperative facilities would be available whenever he required them.

Had he done this we would not have been able to make our legitimate claim to our insurance company as compensation for the loss of his services after having paid out the £1.35m fee.

In the event he agreed that it was potentially impossible for him to continue in professional football and as we parted company we handed him a cheque for £250,000 as an ex gratia payment.

Another transfer that caused me a great deal of irritation was, rather oddly, the movement of a player between two clubs in a foreign country. This was when David Platt went from Bari to Juventus in June 1992, a year after he had left Villa Park in his record signing for Bari.

When Platt left Villa Park part of the agreement was that we would receive half of any profits if and when he was sold on, but when that situation arrived I'm certain that a spot of tactical planning went on which cost us some £1.25m.

The figure quoted to us for Platt's resale was £5.5m, the same figure Bari had paid. All very convenient. However, I established that two players, Allessio and Di Uri had moved from Juventus to Bari on top of the fee, taking the actual value of the move to an estimated £8m. Thus Bari's profit amounted to £2.5m of which we were entitled to receive half.

To this end I appealed to Signor Mattarese to meet our agreement.

Receiving no response I then took on the services of a lawyer in Italy who appeared to be putting the necessary case together for us to appeal through UEFA and FIFA, when out-of-the-blue he telephoned me to say that he could no longer pursue his inquiries. He would not explain why, not on the telephone and that was the last I heard from him.

My next move was a further appeal to Signor Mattarese, reminding him of the excellent relationships we had previously enjoyed when Gordon Cowans and Paul Rideout moved between our clubs. In reply to this I received a remarkable fax message from the Bari president saying that if I continued with the process 'he feared for my future'. Naturally incensed at what seemed a thinly-veiled threat I recall ringing Ron Atkinson at the training ground to discuss what we should do next. There was a brief silence and then a hoot of laughter. "I would leave it alone if I were you, chairman," chortled Ron, or something like that. "Otherwise you could find yourself wearing a concrete overcoat and holding up an Italian motorway." Bearing in mind that Signor Mattarese is said to produce about half of the cement used throughout Italy I decided to take Ron's advice though, as a last throw, took a second opinion from the Chief Constable, who said he would make inquiries. One week later he recommended that I should 'forget it'.

It became crystal clear to me during the club's close-season tour of South Africa in 1994 that there was no way that Ron Atkinson and I would ever forge a constructive working relationship in moving the club forward. The Coca Cola Cup win should have been the basis for a period of consistent success. Just think about the opportunity which existed: we had returned to European competition, financial stability was there in terms of resources, available for the right kind of signings and a large enthusiastic support was bursting to help us achieve more honours. All working together there is nothing we could not have achieved.

Sadly, the reality was very different. The only communication between the manager and myself came as a result of my contacting him. It was never the other way around. On that tour, where he was accompanied by his wife, it was very evident to me that he desired no manager-chairman relationship whatsoever if he could avoid it.

His rapport with players seemed to me to be equally selective in terms of there being certain senior players whom he favoured and treated one way and others with whom he was far more distant. Dalian Atkinson was, for instance, the one and only player who could get away with back-chatting and wise-cracking with the manager, sometimes I felt in a way which other players could have resented bearing in mind how, unlike Dalian, they had to be very careful what they said and did.

All this I could just about have handled had team affairs been successful or even satisfactory. Quite distinctly, as the disappointing season progressed, they were not.

Premiership results in the closing weeks of the previous season, dating right back to the Coca Cola Cup semi-final success over Tranmere Rovers had been continuously poor.

True, season 1994-95 started encouragingly enough with three draws and two victories in the opening five Premiership fixtures leading up to the UEFA Cup-tie against Inter Milan.

The home leg win over Inter, with the nerve-wracking penalty shoot-out was one of the many highlights of Ron's time at Villa Park but, worryingly, league results then went into serious decline.

Without wishing to rake over too many unfortunate memories, I have to point out that the record books show us that the squad which the manager insisted was capable of finishing among the top six, had taken just one point from a possible twenty-four up to the fateful night of November 9th when we played Wimbledon at Selhurst Park.

At that time we were 19th in the Premiership with only ten points from 13 games, one place behind our opponents. With some half-hour to go in that game we were leading 3-1 and apparently looking at a victory that might just have been the turning point of the season.

Before half-time Andy Townsend had been sent off, somewhat harshly we all felt, but the ten men remaining ought to have been well capable of defending a potentially winning lead after scoring their third goal early in the second half.

However, in the last half-hour we virtually came apart at the seams and were left looking at a 4-3 defeat and a record of one draw and eight defeats in nine games. Dreadful.

Had I been able to have regular, constructive meetings with the manager to openly discuss any problems he had, make signings, support whatever constructive changes he wished to bring about then maybe we could have halted our alarming slide towards possible relegation. As it was time was running out and I was more likely to see Ron Atkinson on television explaining where other teams were going wrong than sit over a quiet drink with him and talk about Aston Villa's failings.

More than one supporter and shareholder had talked to me critically at that time about Ron's TV work and his capacity to recognise the shortcomings in other teams when our own was losing match after match.

After that defeat by Wimbledon I didn't sleep too well. The fact was that if the other directors felt as I did at an emergency Board Meeting I had called at Villa Park next day, then the manager's hours, let alone days, were numbered. In the event their feelings were totally unanimous, as fellow directors Tony Alderson, the late Dr David Targett and my son Peter Ellis expressed precisely similar misgivings to my own.

I was asked afterwards how I felt about dismissing a manager with such a high public profile, one with a big following among grass-roots supporters, one who had led us to a Coca Cola Cup victory only the previous season, one who was so liked and admired by all sections of the media.

My answer to that was that while it is never pleasant telling a professional man that he has lost his job I was more certain that this one was the correct course of action than any of the previous managerial sackings that had earned me that certain nickname.

Once the decisions had been discussed openly by the board, proposed and carried, I asked my secretary to telephone him and request that he attend a meeting at Villa Park as soon as he could get to us.

When he arrived I called him into the boardroom and, with no need to beat about the bush, informed him that it was the unanimous decision of the Aston Villa board that his contract be terminated in order that we could seek a new manager.

It was a very brief meeting. I honestly believe he was taken completely by surprise, though I personally felt that the case for his departure was beyond dispute. It seemed to the board that if he carried on as manager we would be relegated. I never changed that view and nothing about his subsequent period as a manager at Coventry City and more recently Sheffield Wednesday undermined my judgment. Indeed, as events later unfolded, I had numerous strangers approach me to say that, while they fiercely opposed the sacking of Ron Atkinson when it happened, they later came to appreciate that it had actually proved to be in the best interest of Aston Villa.

Odd, too, that he presumably rediscovered his appetite for travelling from Worcestershire to Sheffield, though this proved merely to be until the end of the 1997-98 season when his contract was not renewed.

Anyway, we sincerely placed on record our appreciation of the successes he had brought to the club and were disappointed that his reign was no longer working out. As in the case of his predecessors we were ready to settle his contract, less an amount to cover tax requirements, there and then. He could have gone home with the appropriate cheque in his pocket.

For whatever reason he declined this offer in favour of asking his accountant to deal with the matter and this, of course, meant that we simply carried on paying him his monthly cheque until the settlement was agreed. He is the only Aston Villa manager, in my time as chairman, who has opted to stretch the matter out in this way and this, of course, was his contractual right.

More pressing matters were now on the agenda. The season was approximately one-third elapsed, relegation was threatening and Aston Villa were, once again, managerless with our supporters roughly split into two 'camps'. On one side there were those who supported the view that it was right for Ron Atkinson to be replaced and, on the other, there were many who were incensed at his departure.

The media, by and large, fell into the latter category though reporters, radio and newspaper reporters are, inevitably, influenced to some degree by a manager's past record and by the amount of co-operation they receive from him and the headlines he inspires.

What sort of successor could adequately fill Big Ron's shoes?

Chapter Fifteen

The Job's Yours, Brian

Not for the first time during my quarter of a century association with Aston Villa FC I found myself plunged into an avalanche of controversy, this time over the dismissal of Ron Atkinson. If the critics were right and I was wrong then we had shamefully discarded their charismatic leader, a larger-than-life character who would guide us forward to ever greater triumphs. On the other side of the coin, if the Board happened to be right and the fiercest of the critics badly wrong then our change at the helm had not been made one moment too soon. The latter scenario was my own unshakeable opinion.

As I have indicated before, you tend to find as a general rule that if things are going well at a club the manager is a genius. When affairs go the other way then the public wants the chairman's head to roll.

Looking back to that particular period, however, I still find it ironic that for all the cast-iron evidence to the contrary there were still those who felt that the manager had the playing affairs of the club on the right lines.

This conveniently overlooked the number of players we had who were operating on what, in Premiership footballing terms, were ageing legs plus the smaller number who were not giving the necessary level of performance. Results are the bottom line of any manager's account and Ron's had been awful for a considerable time.

As for choosing someone to replace him I was totally certain that I would do so without even trying. To be absolutely honest I mentally had my new manager lined up even before Ron Atkinson was fired.

What the dissenting supporters, many of them clamouring to get their letters published in the Birmingham *Evening Mail,* were not to know was that I had known for the previous three years that Brian Little wanted to become manager of Aston Villa as and when the next opportunity arose.

I knew beyond doubt that when he became aware that the job was vacant his interest would be sparked, just as it had been in the summer of 1991, before Atkinson succeeded Jo Venglos. If folks wondered why I appeared, in the circumstances, to be keeping a very low profile that was the reason. Brian Little would be our next manager. It was only a question of the date and the terms of his contract.

How could I be so sure? Simply because he had telephoned me for a little advice a few days before we appointed Ron Atkinson in the summer of 1991. Brian had been approached by Leicester City but wondered if he stood a chance at Villa Park, the job he most wanted.

By this time Atkinson was our choice, but in any event I advised Brian to take the job at Filbert Street in order to add to the experience he had gained with Darlington. To this I added a crucial final promise that was to become the essential basis of my confidence that he would succeed Atkinson.

"If the vacancy occurs again and you remain interested then you have my absolute assurance that you will be considered for it," I told him in 1991. "You will not even have to apply, I will remember." It was that particular sentence that held the key to the controversy which subsequently raged about whether or not we made a wrongful approach to him in November 1995. Bluntly, we did not. We didn't even need to. Brian Little already knew that he was under consideration if he wished to be.

In the event we went through the normal procedure of advertising the vacancy in a national newspaper and this produced some fifty replies.

About thirty of these could be instantly discarded as being from applicants with no previous experience of managing a professional football club. The other twenty included some well-known names and despite what might have appeared in the newspapers at that time we did not interview anyone, much less offer any of them the job even though we were dangerously managerless. In the short-term we had the assistant manager, Jim Barron, in charge of team affairs and, typical of such situations, we went to White Hart Lane for our next fixture, on the Saturday week (November 19th) and reversed the seven-goal Wimbledon scoreline for our first victory in ten Premiership matches.

DEADLY!

By now I had made a formal request to the Leicester City chairman, Martin George, for permission to approach their manager. This request was refused, leaving the ball distinctly in Brian's court.

What now? To my relief it didn't take long for the promise I had given to Brian three years earlier to take affect. Through an intermediary, a reporter to be precise, I was sounded out as to whether his Villa appointment could be guaranteed, subject to contractual agreements if he decided to leave Leicester City. The assurance went back to him that it could, depending on discussions and the approval of the entire board.

As a result of that assurance Brian Little chose to walk out on Leicester City and the following day he spoke to me for the first time.

I invited him to my home in Four Oaks for 'secret' discussions about wages and conditions, well away from the prying eyes and ears of the media, or so I thought.

The discussions took us about an hour, but what we didn't know was that photographers and reporters were hidden away near my home and Brian was pictured getting out of his distinctive four-wheel-drive vehicle on my drive and also my front door being opened to him.

News of his impending appointment was thus virtually common knowledge via local radio and newspapers before our contract talks had even been completed. One thing I had learned long, long before was to never under-estimate the probing powers of the press. They don't miss a lot, believe me. Indeed, as 'neutrals' they can often be quite useful as middle men.

However, all that truly mattered to me was that I now had my tenth, and hopefully my last manager on board, in whom to entrust the playing affairs of Aston Villa FC. Subsequent attempts by Leicester City to slap an injunction on his working for us and/or to bring the wrath of the FA or the FA Premiership down around our ears were abortive, simply because Brian had merely exercised his right to leave one employer and apply for a post with another. In due course two other ex-Villa players, namely his assistant manager Allan Evans and his coach John Gregory also left Filbert Street to rejoin Brian at Villa Park.

There have been many difficult searches for a new manager under my chairmanship but, for all the controversy that stretched on for weeks, this one was the easiest to both decide and to implement.

One significant factor in Brian being appointed to the job he so badly wanted was the input by the club's former commercial manager, Eric

Woodward, whose ex-secretary, Heather, is Mrs Little, the manager's devoted and supportive wife. Eric rang me on several occasions each time we were seeking a new man to commend Brian to me.

Constantly Eric stressed that beneath his courteous and friendly exterior there was a band of steel, a stubborn determination to achieve his objectives in life. Since his cruel injuries that ended his magnificent playing career at the age of 27 he had, bit by bit, taken on board a whole range of impressive qualifications.

As a starting point, Eric claimed, the former star forward was a true Villa man whose allegiance to the club since his days as an apprentice had never wavered. When he finished as a player he spent a spell on the commercial side, including time as a lottery agent along with Abdul Rashid, now himself the commercial manager.

Also, he had talked to Eric about press and public relations and had generally shown an interest in wider matters than playing affairs. Added to this was a spell as a Villa youth team coach, a period as coach and team manager for Wolverhampton Wanderers and then further experience coaching for Middlesbrough when Bruce Rioch was manager at Ayresome Park. As his own man he had sampled relegation from the Fourth Division of the Football League to the Vauxhall Conference in the role of manager of Darlington, followed by a return to the Fourth Division and promotion to the Third.

It was at that point in his career that his advice from myself was to accept Leicester City's offer and learn the ropes at a higher grade, which he did by steering them to Wembley play-offs and into the Premiership.

Eric rightly saw this as the ideal managerial CV and nothing I witnessed in Brian's early years at Villa Park contradicted that judgment. On day one, for instance, he had the players in a circle around him at the training ground when a particular individual arrived late, wearing an American baseball cap backwards and hovering on the fringe of things, perhaps his normal practice.

As the story filtered through to me the new boss took him aside, informed him that if he were late again it would prove very expensive and to remove his inappropriate headgear. Players saw clearly that they could not take liberties with him and this applied to ALL players, with no selected exceptions. Life changed very quickly, I'm led to believe, at the Bodymoor Heath training ground, though it was my rule to be rarely there to see for myself. The training ground is not my immediate responsibility.

Villa Park is my domain, where a shift in routine, and manager-chairman relations, was equally evident, I was delighted to discover. After morning training each day the new manager's set routine was to move to his office at Villa Park and from there, assisted by Allan Evans, to conduct his wider duties. How very different to his elusive and uncommunicative predecessor.

At last there was a sensible, regular rapport in a relaxed atmosphere with the feeling of supporting each other to pull in the same direction.

Quite naturally I waited with interest to discover how he assessed the playing staff, which had begun the season being tipped by Ron Atkinson and as I recall, Alex Ferguson, as being of top-six calibre. It was a fairly brief wait.

Before very long Brian informed me that he was deeply disappointed with the strength of his squad of players and that, the following season, widespread improvements would be urgently necessary.

To be perfectly fair there were many exceptions to this judgement. Ron Atkinson's replacement was fortunate to take over such excellent players as Dwight Yorke, Mark Bosnich, Ugo Ehiogu, Michael Oakes, Andy Townsend, yes, and 'old man' Macca, the incomparable Paul McGrath.

In the shorter-term, however, fighting off the threat of relegation was the all-embracing priority. In the circumstances he did not wish to undermine the confidence of the players he had inherited by giving his misgivings a public airing.

The records show that he successfully achieved his first objective, no mean feat in itself albeit by a narrow margin, and when this became mathematically certain with a 1-1 draw at Norwich in the final match, we mutually became a touch emotional for the first time.

It reminded me forcibly of the afternoon at Swindon when Graham Taylor's team took us into the old First Division and normal reserves were shed in a tide of relief.

Phase Two beckoned for Brian Little. He was to build his own squad.

Chapter Sixteen

Working In Harmony

The summer of 1995 was a highly important period for the club because now Brian Little had both the freedom and the necessary financial support to illustrate whether or not he could operate successfully in a major club.

Since the previous November, apart from comparatively minor adjustments in his predecessor's squad, he had been operating from match to match, desperately looking for survival points and forging a working relationship with myself and the club as a whole.

By this time he had, as I have already pointed out, expressed deep dissatisfaction with the quality and average age of his first-team players. Some managers in this situation would have metaphorically snatched the cheque book and gone on a shopping spree. Not Brian Little. His modus operandi is far more considered and selective than that.

What especially impressed me was that, unlike some previous managers, he had no hang-ups about discussing his thoughts with others including myself, though he's mentally tough enough to ensure that the final decision on team affairs is always his own.

For example I well recall him coming into my office one afternoon and asking: "What do think about us going for Gareth Southgate from Crystal Palace?" "I've seen him a few times," I responded. "I recall seeing him score one cracking goal. He's a very good player. I'll back you if you want him." Quite possibly he did not truly need my opinion, because I've no doubt by this time he had already made his mind up and done his homework on the player's character. But he was happy to observe the courtesy of asking my opinion and seeking my co-operation. What's more he fully accepted my golden rule that while managers and coaches assess team affairs and nominate players to be sold or signed, it is chairmen and/or chief executives who conduct the financial negotiations.

As a matter of fact long before I became known as 'Deadly' I had, in some quarters, taken on board a quite different nickname. "They ought to call you 'Mr Ten Per Cent'" I was informed by one individual in the game, simply because it has always been my objective to pay at least ten per cent less than any asking price.

Almost without exception I have managed to achieve this, though I must confess that I am never too willing to operate the ten per cent rule the other way. When buying players from Crystal Palace there was always one man to contact and one man only: their then chairman Ron Noades, with whom I had many dealings on various committees.

Any reputation I might have about being a dictator at Villa Park was nothing compared to the way that chairmen like Ron Noades at Selhurst Park and Ken Bates at Stamford Bridge always kept their fingers on the pulse at their particular clubs.

Ron would no doubt have liked to keep a player of Gareth's undoubted quality, but Palace had been relegated and the player wished to leave, so he had little alternative but to talk business. As a result I was quickly able to inform our manager that he could go ahead and meet his man, a deal had been struck. That to me was another example of how the chairman-manager relationship should work as Southgate became our record club signing for £2.25m, though he was not to remain the most expensive for long. Running side-by-side with that deal was another proposed incoming transfer where again there had been a beneficial level of co-operation between us. Dating back a considerable time, from before Ron Atkinson had signed John Fashanu, it was blindingly obvious to all that we needed a new front-line striker. This was not just my view. It was Brian's too, and he was combing through the possibles to find someone of the right age and international-class strengths.

As a result of my position on the FA's International Committee I had fairly regular access to Terry Venables, then the England manager. One day I asked him if, from his knowledge of European football, he could recommend a player who could score us twenty goals a season. "Not easily," was his reply. But he promised to keep us in mind.

Some time later he contacted me to say that he and Bryan Robson, an England coach and by then the new manager of Middlesbrough, had been most impressed with the young Yugoslavian international centre forward of Partizan Belgrade, Savo Milosevic, a leading scorer in European competition.

In addition to having watched him in the flesh they had a video consisting of clips of him in action and they were both very impressed with what they saw. He agreed to send me the video by special delivery on the understanding that if we did not go for the player that we should let him know straight away because Bryan Robson would have then pursued an interest on Middlesbrough's behalf. "I've asked Bryan (Robson) to let you have first refusal because you asked me some time ago," said Venables. "And he's agreed. But if you don't go for him, then he will." When the video arrived the next day I passed it on to Brian Little who had been eager to see it. Some other managers would have recoiled at the thought of following up a player recommended in this way.

Brian's reaction was one of acute interest once he had now seen Milosevic's undoubted talents, albeit on video only. The mention of Partizan Belgrade brought an image to my mind of a tall chap whom I had met while attending UEFA Cup draws in Geneva. I checked for a name in the *European Football Yearbook* (Sports Projects) and I felt sure that the Partizan secretary Zarko Secevic, whose name I found in the publication, was the person whom I had met. Putting a call into the club in Belgrade I was pleased to find that he remembered me also and he quickly confirmed that Milosevic was for sale.

There was just one 'minor' snag. That very day the president of the Italian Serie A club, Parma, had sent his private aircraft to Belgrade to collect Milosevic for talks after a deal had more or less been struck between the two clubs. Unless we were to miss out, we had to move quickly.

"Please get in touch with the player," I urged him. "Ask him not to sign for Parma until he has spoken to us. We will match their terms… We're coming over on the first available flight." Come the time to get off to the airport and Brian Little was still out on the pitch talking to the media about the Southgate deal as the player posed for the usual crop of signing pictures.

When a member of staff was sent out to the manager to inform him that the chairman was waiting for him to set off, little did the reporters whom he left virtually in mid-interview to join me for the Belgrade flight realise that our record fee would be overtaken that very day.

When we arrived at Belgrade airport we were met by Partizan officials to be assured that Savo had taken our 'advice' and not signed for Parma, but that he would not be back in the former Yugoslavia for some four hours.

We were taken to the impressive Partizan Stadium for discussions so that we could work out a package that would be suitable to us both, though this time I'm pretty certain I was not able to observe my 'Mr Ten Per Cent' rule. More likely, I suspect they got more out of us than Parma had been ready to pay. If so you could hardly blame them.

Incidentally, I do recall being shown around their marvellous stadium and seeing a trophy room that makes Liverpool's look under-stocked.

However, the news came into the committee room, where we were still talking, that Savo had now arrived, accompanied by his close friend Igor, a former Yugoslav tennis champion and a sports presenter who appears regularly on their TV screens. The pair were summoned into the meeting and it was very evident to me that players were kept very much 'in their place', rather like it used to be in this country.

During the talks that followed Igor spoke perfect English and took very good care of his pal Savo's affairs. We found Milosevic to be a big, impressive young man who was once an outstanding basketball player.

Soon, after our manager had held discussions with the powerful Serb, helped by Igor, a deal was struck in principle, though we insisted that we would not return the next day without him so that he could see what we had to offer him in terms of facilities and a stage on which to play while also undergoing the necessary medical. This principle was agreed.

By now it was around midnight. It had been a long day. Time for some shut-eye? Indeed not... Our hosts insisted on taking us out for a meal, since none of us had eaten for several hours, and we found ourselves at a restaurant on the outskirts of the city where, to our amazement bearing in mind it was now the wee small hours, the place was alive and buzzing.

It was rather strange to reflect that we were in what had become known as 'War-torn former Yugoslavia', where terrible civil unrest was going on between the rival ethnic factions of Serbs, Croatians and Muslims.

As we sat enjoying a delightful meal and a bottle or two of wine not all that far down the road innocent people were being caught up in the strife and UN mercy missions were having a hard time attempting to restore some stability. It was only later that we learned that one of the reasons Savo wanted the funds that he would accumulate from his £3.5m move was to help move his family from an enclave where they were virtually surrounded by warring groups, to a 'safe haven' flat in Belgrade, where peace reigned.

Eventually we went to bed at about 4am, having arranged to meet Savo and Igor at the airport in good time before our flight.

Brian and I were there in plenty of time. But no Savo. Time ticked away.

Still no Savo. Warning signs began to flash. "Is he going to let us down," we agonised as it got perilously near to departure time.

Panic stations were not too far away, when through the departure lounge strolled Aston Villa's potential record signing, along with Igor, ready to begin what was to become something of a roller-coaster ride in a claret-and-blue shirt.

There was never a moment's doubt in my mind that Brian Little would grow in stature at Villa Park once his first, desperately-difficult season had been completed with the Premiership place successfully defended.

This confidence increased as painstakingly, player-by-player, he dispensed with many of those he had inherited and replaced them, usually with younger models in accordance with our agreed transfer policy.

I mean no disrespect to outstanding players such as our former captain Kevin Richardson, Ray Houghton, Dalian Atkinson, Dean Saunders, Garry Parker, Bryan Small, John Fashanu, Shaun Teale, Earl Barrett, Graham Fenton and Guy Whittingham, but they had been given their chance to consolidate on Villa's League Cup victory and, instead, the club had almost been relegated.

A new manager, as always, wanted his own squad comprising players whom he had selected and signed himself and had introduced into the code of conduct he expects of professional athletes.

The names of the players he recruited are there in the record books and it is interesting to look back and recall that there were seven of his signings in the team which beat Manchester United 3-1 at Villa Park on the opening day.

From there we simply took off and by May 1996 we had regained the Coca Cola Cup with a sparkling Wembley victory over Leeds United, were back in Europe, had reached the semi-final of the FA Cup and were fourth in the FA Premiership.

Brian Little had successfully challenged leading managers in Britain, as I was certain that he would, and I was more than delighted to secure his services on a new contract to keep him at the helm into the 21st century just as he, at that time of current success and encouraging signs for the future, was delighted to stay.

As he himself wrote, without my knowledge at the time I have to say: "I have known the chairman ever since I came into football and I don't think the word 'fear' has ever come into my thinking about anyone, least of all Mr Ellis. I find it quite funny that people call the chairman 'Deadly' and even try to avoid him in some instances. Actually I go out of my way to make sure I see him most days and although I feel it is a very important role for me to play, I can assure all the doubters that it is not an act. The chairman is always interested in my thoughts and I have no worries about relaying those thoughts to him." These were Brian's unsolicited words, not mine, in his book *Return of the Little Villan* (Sports Projects £11.95).

Strange how, despite such public statements from him, folks still jumped to the conclusion that he was 'pushed' when he subsequently left the club, quite against my wishes.

However, back to his happier days at the club, from a season of almost total, non-stop enjoyment at seeing such progress being achieved, one little scenario sticks in my mind and when I describe it maybe it will appear to be a mere ego trip. In reality it was more than that to me, a demonstration that after years of battling, sometimes against pockets of public opinion I had won a place in the hearts and minds of at least some of the supporters and had recovered from the psychological buffeting undergone after dismissing Ron Atkinson.

I had arrived at Wembley for the League Cup Final against Leeds United and was walking up the steps to the main entrance when I heard my name being chanted behind me and turned around to see an army of at least a thousand claret-and-blue bedecked fans.

These people are the lifeblood of the club whom we couldn't function without. Of course we greatly treasure our sponsors, our executive boxholders, our long-serving season ticket holders.

But by and large they are not the people who paint their faces claret-and-blue, who tog up in zany get-ups, who sing the songs, follow the team to every away game, friendlies and all, who spend their last pound of pocket money on the club and who are always there, come what may.

It was a gathering of those sort of supporters who were making music for my ears as they chanted: "There's only one Doug Ellis..." Imagine that! Eighteen months earlier they had been 'Big-Fat-Ron's-Claret-and-Blue Army' until they turned on me as the chairman for having the temerity to dispense with the services of their charismatic leader. It was the change of attitude embodied by that chant that did my heart good. And what a day it proved to be.

At the Cup-winning banquet in central London later that night I had Heidi and the family around me, one very proud man, indeed.

The events of the remainder of that season, with fourth place in the Premiership, achieved following an FA Cup semi-final, confirmed our potential for further progress and also strengthened our resolve to continue the upgrading of Villa Park, which had already been going on for several years.

There is no need for the full details of the various development schemes to be outlined here, but our desire to make the stadium meet the demands of the 21st century was to lead to some most insulting, almost malicious comments being made about Villa Park. To say that I was incensed by certain observations about the appearance of Villa Park, and its adverse impact on the Aston landscape, would be the understatement of the decade bearing in mind the neglected relic of former years.

Some background is necessary to understand the outrage we felt when a controversy about the state of Villa Park exploded in the local press in early April 1997.

Since the post-Hillsborough Lord Justice Taylor Report we, like all other clubs had modernised the stadium, step-by-step to meet the legal requirements of its findings. All work carried out had, obviously, required planning approval and great care had been taken to blend into the local environment, including the nearby stately home, Aston Hall.

We had carefully kept Villa Park as near as possible to its traditional character with external brickwork, while adding modern roofing with matching facias on three sides.

We now had a planning request in to bring the main Trinity Road Stand into line with the other three sides and thus complete a matching four sides of the stadium. Also we made it clear that we wished a subsequent further development of the North Stand which houses the club offices to ultimately bring the ground's all-seater capacity to some 50,000.

Here I must point out that Villa Park does not have the look of the modern, custom-built bowl like, say, Molineux or Derby County's new stadium, Pride Park. Since our ground was originally built in 1897 there is no way it could and, in any case, there are very many people who are proud of the stadium's more traditional appearance. Certainly I am.

Imagine then how we felt when, in delaying permission for us to carry out the Trinity Road improvements in the summer of 1997 pending a detailed plan containing a scheme for the North Stand End, councillors made insulting comments about our stadium. The council's refusal (they called it a deferment!), moreover, to accept the plans submitted to build the extension to the Trinity Road Stand in the Summer of 1997 cost the club more than £600,000 in wasted fabricated steel alone despite, as we understood it, the council's professional planning officers having recommended that our plans be approved.

The planning committee chairman was quoted in the local press as describing Villa Park as 'an ugly mess' and 'a hotch-potch of four different sheds'. Another official was quoted as saying that Villa Park spoiled the appearance of the vicinity when viewed from the nearby Aston Expressway between Spaghetti Junction and the Birmingham City Centre. Surely, most people who have driven that stretch of road and glanced past Aston Church steeple to Villa Park would not feel that the stadium spoiled the view? The disgraceful phrase 'Ugly Mess' was a banner headline in the *Evening Mail* on Thursday April 3rd, hardly the publicity we expected as a result of applying for permission to spend yet another £3.4m on improving the West Midlands' best-known and most historic football stadium.

This, remember, is a stadium which the Football Association has regularly chosen for FA Cup semi-finals, and certainly will do again, and which attracted huge praise from all sides when Euro 96 matches, in the European Championships, were so successfully staged. Anyone following the progress of Villa Park's gradual redevelopment during the 1980s and 1990s and recalling the tumbledown, antiquated decay of 1969, when the first flotation took place, would possibly regard the abusive language to which I have referred as being grossly out of order.

Our only course of action was to meet the council's request to provide a more detailed scheme, outlining our intentions for the North Stand development alongside the Trinity Road plan, while leaving the public at large to decide for themselves on the quality and appearance of the ground and its impact on the local environment. The eventual cost of bringing the stadium capacity up to 50,000 seats was calculated at more than £16m.

All of which reminds me of the new National Stadium that never got off the ground...

Chapter Seventeen

National Stadium Fiasco

In recent years the game of Fantasy Football has become a popular pastime, so why not join me in a game of Fantasy Football Stadiums...? As a member of the FA Council and the International and Finance Committees I increasingly became disgusted with the commercial arrangements for major matches at Wembley Stadium.

Due to a long-standing contractual agreement Wembley Stadium plc took, in my view, a disproportionate amount of the commercial income from internationals, cup finals, replays, promotion play-offs and the like.

Not only this but Wembley could not offer the quality of facilities that the modern-day spectator quite reasonably demands and this includes getting to and from the stadium without unacceptable delays.

Wembley's very location is all against the arrival and departure of large crowds and lines of motor vehicles as anyone who has experienced the problem will testify. Those who live in the south-east can just about put up with the traffic jams and the pressure on public transport because they at least are otherwise reasonably close to home.

Those who have to drive a hundred miles and maybe twice that far once they are eventually clear of the stadium and that, remember, could be after a night match, find that getting to and from Wembley is an absolute nightmare.

It can easily take a couple of hours getting out of the car park and thus it is turned midnight before they even commence the drive home. The whole infrastructure around the stadium conflicts with the requirements of seventy-odd thousand people and it is difficult to see how they can make truly significant improvements. The last time Aston Villa played in the Coca Cola Cup Final, against Leeds United, in March 1996, our staff coaches took over two hours to get to the stadium, the short distance from their hotel in the West End of London and they arrived at their seats only just in time to see the kick-off. This sort of thing has been going on for years. When we drew against Everton in the 1977 League Cup Final on a Saturday afternoon, a banquet was staged at the Metropole Hotel near the National Exhibition Centre just outside Birmingham. By the time all the coaches had fought their way through miles and miles of traffic all the way from the stadium the function had been delayed late into the evening and was as good as ruined.

Even the official FA party for major matches is affected as badly as the long-suffering public at large. We leave from White's Hotel, Bayswater Road, near the FA headquarters in Lancaster Gate and we have to give ourselves two hours at least. Getting back is even worse unless you wait at the stadium for a couple of hours to allow the traffic to ease.

It has been interesting to note that certain London writers, who tend to be defensive about anything concerning the capital, have written newspaper articles expressing doubts about whether Wembley is the ideal location for our national stadium of the future, which it manifestly is not.

OK, now to 'dream up' that Fantasy Football Stadium, not just for those who live in London and its surrounds, but for the benefit of the national and international football family in its entirety.

The location must be central to suit the majority. The site needs to be adjacent to a motorway network feeding all directions, near an international airport and railway station and on a large rural site with plenty of car parking space. In addition, massive capital funds must be available plus a blueprint that would suit all of the FA Premiership clubs and other potential users of what would be one of the finest, most ideally-situated stadiums in Europe?

Fantasy satisfied? Well, this scenario, dear reader, was not fantasy, but potentially a feasible proposition had there existed the will to put the scheme into operation. I argued in FA Council that football was a working man's game with its roots in the north of England, Scotland, the Midlands and elsewhere.

With this in mind a state-of-the-art stadium to accommodate 85,000 people from all points of the compass, in comfort, with plenty of leg room had become absolutely essential and that the centre of England was the logical site for it.

A green site where environmental considerations could be met alongside all the other requirements of convenient travel was the obvious location and we had such a proposal adjacent to the National Exhibition Centre which, because of its own huge success, has simply grown and grown. A new stadium nearby would surely prosper in similar fashion.

The £100m plan which our Midland-based group put forward was for the stadium to be in a bowl with part of it submerged below ground level so as to be concealed from view.

It was immediately adjacent to the M42 leading to the M40, M5 or the M6-M69 and the M1, roughly an hour's easy drive to the outskirts of London, Manchester, Liverpool and Sheffield, a stone's throw from Birmingham International airport and a London-line railway station and with ample car park space to accommodate 30,000 vehicles. There was a moving walkway scheme direct to the railway station where additional platform space would be provided and speedy access to the airport. A running-water moat would surround the stadium which would be built in 110 acres with a third of the seats sunken below ground level.

Part-funding would come from the sum of £40m spread over five years to be provided by the members of the Premier League who would thus have a vested interest. When I put this financial proposition to the Premier clubs at their monthly meeting on two occasions there were no dissensions from my chairman colleagues.

Also I was quite confident that the remaining £60m would be forthcoming from lottery funds over a similar period, because of the number of sporting and leisure activities for which such a magnificent stadium could be used, including major music concerts.

There were massive business opportunities for the surrounding West Midlands commercial community, including Solihull whose planning permission was required. We had gone deeply into the possible annual usage and turn-over with the conclusion that the scheme was entirely viable.

Yet, incredibly, when our project was considered along with one from Manchester and that of upgrading Wembley stadium it was rejected by the Sports Council on the grounds that planning permission for the site had not been forthcoming.

Let me just examine this 'excuse'. I had met The Birmingham City council, along with Rick Parry, chief executive of the FA Premier League. The Deputy Leader, Councillor Bryan Bird had expressed the view that his Labour colleagues in Solihull would support the scheme, with all its multitude of benefits for the locality.

I had taken the precaution of also enlisting the presence of Graham Shaylor, Birmingham's retired chief planning officer and temporary chief executive of the City Council, to act as a consultant. We felt we were very well on the way to bringing the scheme to fruition. True, our planning application to Solihull had originally been rejected on the grounds of increased traffic, but the usual procedure for planning permission to build on greenbelt land necessitates it being called in by the appropriate Minister who appoints an inspector to thoroughly investigate all the relevant factors. In cases where a national interest is involved, as was the case here, a local rejection can be overturned. I was confident that this is how it would have worked out. Had we been given the necessary six months breathing space to get the application called in by the Minister, we would have won.

However, to reach that stage the Sports Council would have needed to include us among the possibles. This they failed to do. I wonder why...? Certainly, to be thrown out at the first hurdle, as unbelievable lobbying for Wembley Stadium went on behind the scenes, was absolutely heart-breaking. I was left with the very firm impression that we had lost out to political influences, i.e. the London Mafia, just as Birmingham's excellent Millennium Celebration scheme, with its structure already in being, was defeated by a rubbish dump in Greenwich.

So, will the proposed 'new' Wembley come into being and justify the decision? Only time and traffic jams would tell, but even if a satisfactory stadium finally emerges the location will be unacceptable to a large section of the football community. Not one to give up the fight too easily I made it known to Graham Kelly in the April of 1998, when it became known that Arsenal had ditched plans to possibly play at Wembley, and the stadium's future remained unclear, that the centre of England project still remained an option. If it were backed with the full-weight of approval from all interested parties, planning permission could be obtained, of this I remain confident.

Possessing a stadium fit for the next century is one important issue. Preparing the England team to live up to its splendour is even more desirable and this aspect comes firmly under my wing as chairman of the

Football Association's technical control board, the body which supports Howard Wilkinson, the Director of Coaching, in his task of improving the nation's skills for future years.

In this particular capacity my belief is that as far as individual skills are concerned arising from our methods of coaching youngsters, we are light years behind major European football countries, especially Holland and France plus others including Germany. This was why our committee, representing the FA, put our weight solidly behind the proposals to transform the old United States Air base at Upper Heyford in Oxfordshire into a magnificent multi-purpose British Academy of Sport incorporating a national football academy.

Unhappily the subject, like the national stadium, then became a political football, when Chris Smith, Labour's Culture and Sport Secretary talked of excluding 'team sports' such as football, cricket and rugby from the academy plans, before having second thoughts and talking of centres of excellence all around the country.

At the time of writing the topic is thus regrettably shrouded in controversy and political in-fighting, just at a time when the need becomes more pressing to meet the continentals on a level playing field in terms of nurturing outstanding young footballers from a very early age.

The Sheffield bid, which is an excellent one, was the one to be accepted so whatever the eventual outcome of the decisions reached I wish to go on record as stating quite categorically that from football's standpoint Upper Heyford is a heaven-sent location for a National Academy.

The US Air Force left behind outstanding and varied facilities, in good condition, including a sixty-bed hospital and many useful amenities. In addition to this a hundred acres of valuable space could be allocated to football pursuits on the old airfield. Also, the potential deal with the Oxfordshire local authority was favourable in the shape of a 99-year lease on a peppercorn rent subject to receiving a grant from the National Lottery of £30m to provide capital and maintenance.

Along with Howard Wilkinson and our FA colleagues we firmly believed the location, with all the facilities that could be created there, was ideal for producing young footballers with the quality and calibre to bring England up to the level of the best in Europe and the World.

What I thought was a good opportunity to convince the Government of the benefits of Upper Heyford ahead of the Lilleshall and Sheffield projects came in Paris last summer when Tony Banks, the Minister for

Sport and myself, attended the Final of Le Tournoi between England and Brazil. I gave him a lengthy ear-bending on the subject and was very hopeful that it would have an effect until Chris Smith's comment cast doubts about that and Sheffield won the day.

The fact is that we have continued to fall behind the other major footballing nations in terms of scientific preparation of young players, as I realised forcibly when attending France's National Academy at Clair Fontain, near Paris. It is a magnificent establishment with every conceivable aid to teaching young players the basic skills and then building on them as they, the Dutch, the Germans and others have continued to do, sometimes to our embarrassment.

To encapsulate my personal feelings of total frustration about the dual situation, let me sum up what might have been: one of the finest football stadiums in the world situated in the very centre of the nation and with a magnificent Academy of Sport, equipped to employ every modern technique, a comparatively short drive away. All of this in easy reach of London and with a viable financial package on hand to bring it all to fruition.

What other enlightened nation in the whole world would need second thoughts about integrating such a package? If those nations proceed to show greater technique than we do and to beat us in the international arenas perhaps, as a nation, it is our own fault? In any event, so much for Football Association matters. My first concern would always be Aston Villa FC. And flotation talk was soon to be in the air.

Chapter Eighteen

Ups And Downs Of Flotation

A lady of mature years walked into the Birmingham office of stockbrokers Albert E Sharp in the Spring of 1997, produced a sheaf of Aston Villa share certificates and asked how much they were worth.

The charming lady had read that, with a flotation underway, Villa shares had sharply risen in value. It sounded like very good news to her as one of the club's thousands of long-standing shareholders.

Her late father had left her with a substantial holding, though until reading recent newspaper reports, it had not occurred to her that they were anything but paper value. As it transpired, however, the growth of the club over the years meant that she had a pleasant surprise in store.

The clerk who perused the share certificates suggested that she should come inside, sit down and enjoy a cup of tea while a more senior member of staff was summoned to discuss her shareholding with her.

What were they now worth with the stock exchange flotation looming, she had asked? The member of staff called up a more senior colleague to break the news.

"Are you sitting comfortably, madam?" he asked, or words to that effect.

"Your shares, being Special Shares, are worth an estimated £1.3m.

"Madam, are you all right? Would you like another cup of tea?" Our fortunate if speechless lady was in fact Mrs Barbara Nation and the news of her windfall was extremely nostalgic to my ears dating back, as it did, to the momentous affairs of 1968.

Mrs Nation's late father was Joe Heath, a self-made local businessman

157

and one of the Villa directors who had forfeited his place to make way for my new administration in that eventful December 1968 upheaval.

Joe, a friend of mine, was the person who supported Bruce Normansell's vain proposal to have me elected to the board back in 1964, the episode I have written about earlier.

In a way this anecdote is a financial barometer of the 29 years between the two flotations. The value of those bits of paper, purchased by supporters of all income groups as an illustration of their commitment to the club, had multiplied in value by several thousand times.

Those who bought one share for a fiver, for instance, found that, at the market peak their share certificate was now worth £1,100 and a 'Special Share' was fifteen times that value.

Subsequently it was a fact that, after the 1997 flotation, share values went down very significantly along with the others in the same sector, and confirmed fears I had always held that the clubs who floated before us set their figures too high to the detriment of those who were to follow. Indeed, let me be quite explicit in confirming that for quite a while I was deeply sceptical about the whole idea.

The start of it all was Manchester United's decision to 'go public', followed by a similar move by Tottenham Hotspur. As a result we began to get approaches from banks and financial institutions, but in principle I still remained profoundly unsure.

City eyes had been attracted towards football by the turn-over increases that such as ourselves had achieved from around £13m a year to an escalating £30m a year, supplemented by unprecedented stadium improvements, the BSkyB TV contract, other commercial interests and a general upsurge in the sport's following. The purging of the old hooligan problem by modern-day security measures was another positive influence.

The first individual to begin my gradual transition towards the idea was Adam Shutkeever, an exceedingly bright barrister, young diehard Aston Villa supporter, originally from Birmingham, representing Deutsche Morgan Grenfell, the German owners of the big finance house. He wrote to me and visited me at Villa Park outlining his estimate of the current stock market value of Aston Villa FC. This he and a colleague whom he brought along, set at substantially over £100m, probably double the figure I would personally have placed on the club at that time. Bear in mind that, since I have never had any intention whatsoever of selling any significant part of my Aston Villa holding, and certainly of never putting the club up for auction, talk of the club's paper value was of no more than passing concern.

I wrote back to each of the brokers who had approached us to say that I was not interested in a flotation at this time and, indeed, said as much to shareholders at the Annual General Meeting of August, 1996. I was asked from the floor at that AGM if it were my intention to float and my perfectly truthful answer was that it was not. Basically I was concerned about the treadmill that one could get onto whereby the banks, investment houses, brokers, whatever, are telling you how to run the club.

Nevertheless, the city's interest in us persisted and since we were to invest more large capital sums into stadium improvements and also needed to give Brian Little further support in the transfer market, the possibility of substantial cash injections into our funds could not be ignored. Consequently, when we visited Old Trafford on New Year's Day, 1997, I made it my business to glean what information I could about Manchester United's experiences as a Public Limited Company and the various, complicated procedures involved.

My misgivings at the danger of possibly outlandish values being placed on clubs and their share price listings had led to my making an unscheduled visit to Sir John Hall who, by now, had agreed to float Newcastle United. Press reports suggested that Newcastle were to float at what I felt was far too high a figure. Two hundred million pounds was being suggested as their likely figure. The mechanics of going public are less complicated than some might imagine.

Basically a valuation is set and divided up into the relevant number of shares, at whatever individual price is selected, and then the stock markets sell them to institutions and individuals at an increasing or decreasing price as the markets fluctuate. Were clubs to over-value themselves, and thus the price of their shares, would we be in danger of 'killing the goose that was laying the golden eggs'? I was afraid that we would. In order to make my concerns known I called on Sir John at a hotel where he was staying in London and got him out of bed for an informal but, I felt, a profoundly important chat.

It was well after midnight when he was eventually able to return to his bed but, by the time he had turned in for a second time that night, I felt I had convinced him of the dangers of going for a sum far in excess of what financial advisers might set as the club's realistic market value.

My view was that over-pricing in this way could crucially affect the performance of others in the football sector. In the long-term it could be extremely detrimental to us all and I never reversed this view.

I asked Sir John to reconsider his valuation and go for £160m. This, I suggested, would result in a massive over-subscription while retaining his share price rather than have them selling at a discount, i.e. less than their original value on flotation day.

A rapid fall in price cannot be a favourable outcome, I stressed.

However, a club like ours could not be seen to be floating at a massively lower figure than others of similar financial potential.

When I left Sir John, with whom I have had an amicable relationship for some years, I felt that I had convinced him of my theory.

Readers may feel that I was a touch presumptuous in approaching him in this way but, in fact, when he first became chairman of Newcastle United he asked me if he could visit Villa Park to see how a football club should be run. He asked for two hours of my time but, after flying down to Birmingham, he was with us for double that period. Thus, in some measure we had contributed to his building the St James's Park club as it has since become. With this in mind I had no qualms in seeking him out in an attempt to dissuade him from over-capitalising on the market valuation issue since their price would inevitably affect ours and others.

In the event Sir John took only limited account of my advice and lowered his figure from £200m to £193m. History now tells us that my fears were realised and that the Newcastle shares were soon selling at a substantially discounted price. For whatever reason, Sir John retired for a while until the headline-hitting problems at St James's Park led to him returning to the helm at a time when the club's place in the Premiership was under threat, along with share prices.

So why did we eventually decide on a flotation ourselves? The men who finally convinced me were Martin Edwards, the chairman of Manchester United FC and Sir Roland Smith, the chairman of Manchester United plc during that Old Trafford visit for a 0-0 draw on New Year's Day 1997.

Sir Roland Smith was formerly chairman of British Aerospace, Rover and several other well-known companies. By now I had been approached by some ten financial houses and had seen three of them at their request but had retained many of my original misgivings.

However, Martin Edwards assured me that he had been assailed by similar doubts as myself, but after being persuaded to go for it he had discovered that the process had been less troublesome than he had imagined and that he now enjoyed and appreciated Manchester United's status on the stock exchange and his periodic visits to financial institutions involved.

Sir Roland then took me aside in their spacious and luxurious board-room and observed that, having known me for many years, I would also actually enjoy the change and that Aston Villa would unquestionably reap meaningful benefits. He had no doubts that we could handle the transition without any undue worries or difficulties. We should go ahead. That was the Manchester United advice, and I took it, not without a sense of history when I recalled the rather less spectacular flotation of 1969.

The one important proviso was the very same that I had offered to Sir John Hall, namely to keep the price down as low as possible compared to other clubs in a similar situation, to allow for the possibility of shares increasing in value rather than being sold at a discount. Sir Roland also recommended the Birmingham brokers Albert E Sharp to handle the operation and I have to say that this proved to be very sound advice.

After the necessary lengthy discussions and outline planning the arrangements we put into force set our Market Cap, as it is known, at between £120m and £140m. This would have created a competitive market and would almost certainly have resulted in shares increasing in value but for one powerful, adverse force which we had not anticipated.

None of us, not Albert E Sharp, nor anyone at the club, imagined that the original 8,000 shareholders dating back to the 1969 flotation would sell their shares as they did.

The trend that emerged, and I have to repeat that it took us by surprise, was that our existing shareholders, a high proportion of them season ticket holders, cashed in on their investment to the extent of a £1,000 each, while holding on to a reduced number. Unfortunately one of the directors I had invited onto Aston Villa's board in the early 1970s, who had purchased £25,000-worth of shares, sold some of them for a very handsome profit. Similarly the little old lady whose father had invested £30,000 in Villa shares, sold most of hers for a million pounds; two transactions that seriously added to the discounting of our share value.

It was this that made it a seller's, rather than a buyer's market, forcing the value of our shares down in a manner which I had tried so carefully to avoid. As one shareholder put it to me: "This has paid for my season ticket for the next three years." Obviously, in the context of the flotation, plans for which we announced on February 6th, well in advance of the actual day, the mass profit-making was a big disappointment.

On the other hand it did mean that those who had helped the club all those years ago had now been repaid for their faith beyond their wildest dreams. Since then I've asked well-informed people in the stockbroking business whether they can name another five pound share, in any business pursuit, that cost a fiver and resold for up to £1,600 and all I have received in reply is shaking of heads.

Inevitably, I suppose, there are some who have criticised our flotation. These critics do not include Barbara Nation, and many like her.

Those who put their 1997 shares away and forget them for a few years may find, that just like them, they will receive a pleasant surprise one day in the future. Without going into too much detail it is a fact that 'going public' demands that a company gets its organisation on a very sound footing at all levels especially financially, and with a structured management policy.

To this end we took on a new, executive financial director in Mark Ansell, a chartered accountant who was formerly head of Corporate Finance with Deloitte & Touche, Midlands. A dedicated, lifelong Aston Villa fan, he was an enormous help in advising on the many and varied requirements. We also strengthened the board by the co-opting of two non-executive directors in Tony Hales, the chief executive of Allied Domecq plc and David Owen, a former senior vice-president, who is a senior partner in Edge & Ellison, Aston Villa's long-serving club solicitors.

But the wealth of experience and specialised expertise does not end there. One of our two senior vice-presidents is Mervyn King, a Deputy Governor of the Bank of England who is a close associate of Bank of England number one, Eddie George, the person now responsible, since Gordon Brown became Chancellor of the Exchequer, for adjusting the national bank rate and interest charges. Mervyn King is a fanatical Aston Villa supporter, from his Birmingham University days on the Holte End and who has, for some time, been a regular in our directors' guest room on match days. The other senior vice-president was Lord Howell of Aston Manor, formerly Denis Howell and ex-Labour Minister for Sport and international referee, another big Villa man.

Sadly and tragically, however, within weeks of the flotation, our board strength was reduced by the sudden and totally unexpected death of Dr

David Targett, director and long-serving club physician, a wonderful sportsman, champion of all things claret-and-blue and a dear, dear friend and boardroom colleague.

His death on May 18th, 1997, followed by the death of Lord Howell a year later, set me thinking very deeply about all such people, at various levels of the club who have made such selfless contributions to its health and well-being.

Chapter Nineteen

Losing A Loyal Friend

For some time it was the custom for a friendly group of four of us to travel together to all, or certainly most, of our away games around the country.

Our regular carload would consist of Steve Stride, Dr David Targett, Dr Barrie Smith and myself.

Brian Little's second full season was always in danger of being something of a 'follow that' exercise, given the outstanding achievements of 1995-96, and as our quartet travelled around we saw again and again just how difficult it was to maintain and improve the standards that had been established.

Our defence of the Coca Cola Cup ended at Wimbledon in the fourth round and our attempt to win the FA Cup for the first time for forty years came to grief, also in the fourth round, at Derby.

By then our UEFA Cup return had not survived the first round, as the underrated Swedes of Helsingborgs IF put up the shutters in the second leg at home after a shock late equaliser had given them a 1-1 draw at Villa Park. We were thus left with the Premiership as our one hope of more honours and as our Championship challenge faded, a return to Europe became our only remaining target.

Set against these slightly disappointing affairs were the increasingly encouraging attendances at Villa Park, a sure sign that our public had become as confident as we were behind the scenes that the club's old inconsistencies had finally been banished. Faith in the future had arrived at last.

The season saw our average attendance rise from 32,614 to 36,027 with seven full houses of 39,339 and ten games at which the gate exceeded 30,000. We knew we had to repay such confidence and this gave our campaign to grasp one of the UEFA Cup places on offer an increased importance.

As the pattern at the top of the Premiership and in the domestic cups took shape so it emerged that fifth place in the league would be enough to achieve our objective. Our travelling foursome left after Aston Villa's final visit to the dear old Baseball Ground (replaced in 1997-98 by Pride Park) slightly unnerved by a second away defeat at the hands of Jim Smith's ever-improving Derby County. A home draw with Tottenham Hotspur kept the situation more than a shade tense and after another draw, at Leeds, we arrived at our final away game, against Middlesbrough at their new Riverside Stadium knowing that a victory, or maybe a draw, would clinch that European place. What a day it proved to be, one I shall never forget, for all the wrong reasons, as long as I live.

I had always had it in mind that, since this was our final away game of the season, and would hopefully see our European target achieved, I would arrange a special end-of-the-season, celebration meal for our travelling foursome on the return journey.

The venue was to be a favourite restaurant of mine, the Dovecliffe Hotel, just off the A38 near Burton-on-Trent, a short drive from home, though I deliberately left a decision until after the match. Maybe we would not feel like dining in style if we had not achieved the result we required?

As it transpired the Riverside fixture left us feeling as though our emotions had been put through a spin dryer.

At half-time we were 2-0 down, but then we staged a magnificent second-half recovery as Ugo Ehiogu and Savo Milosevic scored goals to equalise for what looked, until the closing seconds, to be a 2-2 draw.

Then came the mental trauma of a highly debatable decision against us and Ravanelli netted a last-ditch penalty for a 3-2 scoreline in Middles-brough's favour. Bryan Robson's team was fighting, vainly it was to prove, for Premiership survival, so naturally enough their supporters were as delirious as we were deflated.

When we set off for our long drive home I felt that our mood did not make for a cosy restaurant meal. However, you have to learn in football to mentally pick yourself up and, in any case, we justifiably had every confidence that Brian Little and his players would achieve the necessary points for European qualification when we met Southampton, another of the clubs fighting against relegation, in the final match of the season at Villa Park eight days hence.

As we shrugged off our disappointment on the drive back we used our mobile telephone to contact the restaurant and book a table for four. And why not? The whole purpose was to celebrate the fellowship we had enjoyed on our journeys throughout the season, not the result of one match. In a now-convivial frame of mind, and all seemingly in perfect health, we enjoyed our meal and returned to my home where David and Barrie's car had been left for their drive home.

The events of the following few hours left an indelible mark on the club, and certainly on myself. When David arrived home, having said nothing to us about being in any way unwell, he told his wife he had a bad headache and was afraid he was having a brain haemorrhage.

Immediate arrangements were made for him to be admitted to hospital where his self-diagnosis proved to be accurate. On May 18th he passed away having spent his remaining days on a life support machine. I just hope that news of our victory over Southampton got through to him and that he was aware that the European bid had been successful.

As I wrote in the subsequent Chairman's Report to be presented to shareholders at the first annual meeting of the now renamed Aston Villa plc: "David enjoyed all kinds of sport and for many years was involved in boxing and speedway but football, and particularly Aston Villa was always his first love.

"Indeed, his loyalty and support for the club were such that in the early years when the finances were considerably less buoyant than they are today, he received little or no recompense. Professional football, by its nature, is a short-term career, but it is a measure of the affection and respect in which David Targett was held that many of the players he treated and advised down the years remained friends long after their football careers were over.

"Blessed with a wonderful sense of humour and a caring and concerned nature, David was a marvellous colleague and a dear friend to Aston Villa, its directors, players and staff. We all miss him."

Similar sentiments apply to the late Lord Howell, just plain Denis at Villa Park, another lovely man whose heart and soul was in Aston Villa FC. To talk about the positions he occupied and all of his achievements would be a book in themselves. Just one anecdote, recalled by Steve Stride from the European Cup-winning year of 1982, illustrates his service to the club. During the semi-final against Anderlecht in Brussels an English soldier, based out there, had run onto the pitch causing a stoppage.

Subsequently the Belgian club claimed that the stoppage had prevented a possible goal and called for the semi-final leg to be replayed. Denis Howell was chosen as the club spokesman at the UEFA hearing. During the proceedings Denis asked the referee where he restarted the game after the stoppage. The referee's reply was that he restarted the game in the centre circle; to which Denis replied, in best Rumpole fashion: "Well, how could a goal have been threatened, then...?" Obviously one couldn't have been.

Game, Set and Match to Denis Howell and Aston Villa... the latter being freed to beat Bayern Munich in the European Cup Final in Rotterdam.

A true statesman, indeed, and another good friend passed on.

Recording David's and Denis's loyalty to the club in this way reminded me of how many part-time and full-time employees we are fortunate to have who have been with us for many, many years. Could this mean that, behind the scenes, I have been less 'deadly' with Aston Villa staff than I have been with managers who know full-well that they are employed at salaries comparable to the captains of industry on a succeed-or-else basis?

More of that in some detail later, since I am deeply proud of the number of employees who have devoted so much of their working lives to Aston Villa FC under my chairmanship, but first I must recall the events surrounding the record £7m signing of Stan Collymore from Liverpool.

Not all transfers go through in as speedy a fashion as the Southgate-Milosevic deal and the whirlwind twenty-four hours in which they were sorted out. The £7m Stan Collymore signing was a classic example of how sometimes it is necessary for the prey to be stalked with all the patience of a cat after a mouse. When we eventually got him to put pen to paper for yet another new club record fee in the close season of 1997, it ended literally years of his wanting to play for Aston Villa and Villa having him on the wanted list without ever quite getting our collective act together.

If ever a signing illustrated the precarious nature of expensive excursions into the transfer market it proved to be this one, even though it was carried out in good faith and with the best of motives.

The public at large and, indeed, the media has a cut-and-dried attitude towards signing players. They see it as a case of Club A wants Player B, never mind the asking price, the player's terms, the rival bidders and all the other complications, just go sign him. If only it were that simple. And if only the outcome were always as predictable as public and pundits sometimes appear to assume.

Over several years there were many reasons for his arrival at Villa Park being put off but I will always suspect that the final delay, from before the March 1997 deadline for transfers to after the end of the season was caused by our local evening newspaper. What's more, I also suspect, it resulted in the fee we paid to Liverpool increasing by a million pounds.

Successive managers at the club had known about Collymore, who has lived at nearby Cannock just outside Birmingham all his life, from his non-league days with Stafford Rangers and even before that. It is always a shade aggravating to find that, for all the schoolboy and youth coaching carried out by your club, a player of his calibre slips through the net.

However, we tried to sign him in the summer of 1993 when Ron Atkinson offered a package of £1m and three players for him but Barry Fry, who was manager of Southend United at that time, could not afford to pay the three players the kind of money they had been earning at Villa Park. Bearing in mind that in his youth Stan was a devoted Villa fan along with his mates on our famous old Holte End terrace, and that our training ground is a comparatively short drive from his home, it doesn't take much working out that he would have jumped at the move had a deal been worked out. In the event Frank Clark agreed to meet Fry's £2m cash demand and took Collymore to Nottingham Forest where he was a huge success, scoring 41 league goals in 64 appearances.

I would have liked us to sign him before Forest got the chance but our manager wished to stick to a players-plus-cash arrangement, possibly feeling that Collymore was too big a gamble beyond that point and Forest were thus the beneficiaries.

When he was subsequently sold on to Liverpool for £8.5m in August 1995, with Brian Little now our manager, we tried again to sign him, but to be perfectly fair they were in a stronger position at that time and were successful in getting him.

In Liverpool colours he seemed to take a delight in joining with the likes of Robbie Fowler in inflicting upon us some most damaging defeats. Eventually there were hints that Liverpool were prepared to sell him and soundings were being made from Villa Park. Brian Little and I had an offer in at Anfield amounting to £6m, which seemed to be acceptable to them until, in October 1996 the Birmingham *Evening Mail* ran a public poll asking Villa supporters whether or not we should go for Collymore. There was an overwhelming 'yes' vote just as talks between the clubs seemed to be reaching a successful late stage. Then suddenly, coinciding with that pressure of public support for a Collymore signing appearing in the press, there was a change of heart at Anfield where, instead of seeming to us to be on the verge of accepting our approaches, their evaluation of the player increased. Did they see the public pressure as a reason for us to be prepared to substantially increase our terms? That we will never know, though I personally believe it was. But, whatever the reason for it the negotiations went from warm to stone-cold after the *Evening Mail's* ballot and the proposed transfer broke down until it eventually went through on May 13th, 1997.

Collymore arrived at Villa Park amid media discussion about his 'attitude' to his profession, his occasional tendency to skip training and his liking for the Birmingham nightclub scene. Looking back, Brian Little simply saw him as a dynamic goalscorer with the kind of talents he could blend into a team sorely needing them, and was confident of being able to coax the best from him.

In reality there was very little anyone could tell us about Stan, his upbringing and his background, because our former player, chief scout and now reserve team manager, Malcom Beard, has lived near to him and his mother since Stan was a schoolboy footballer and more or less saw him grow up. Malcolm has followed his career and noted his progress as a person throughout the entire period, so we have been kept pretty well informed.

My own first detailed association with our new striker came when, immediately after he had signed for us, Stan joined us on our ten-day end-of-season trip to the United States to play a couple of games during a massive San Francisco Bay British promotion that was being staged there in California and was opened by Prince Andrew who, incidentally, sat by me at the match and impressed me as being very good company.

I found Collymore to be modest, very polite and respectful and also extremely articulate. What's more he turned out to be the only Villa player I have known in nearly thirty years since I first became chairman who has actually bought me a meal. No doubt he will take some stick from his mates for me telling this little story, but I'm sure he can take it.

Whilst in Las Vegas I went out with Dwight Yorke, Ugo Ehiogu, Mark Bosnich and Stan to the huge MGM Grand Hotel with its 5,000 rooms and every possible amenity including, naturally, a casino. The other lads were having a flutter on the machines or tables, as do most visitors, but I've done it all before and Stan did not seem interested in the gambling, either, so when I suggested we go for a meal in a nearby Italian restaurant within the hotel precinct he was all for it, whereas the others seemed to be on a winning streak and preferred to carry on.

We had a pleasant meal, a glass of wine, a friendly chat and when the bill arrived he said: "I will settle that, Mr Ellis." Naturally I protested at first but he insisted: "Please, I would like to pay" and he did. That was, indeed, a whole new experience for me, though I've been the one to pick up the tab on more occasions than I would care to recall with other players, as you can well imagine and as I would expect.

The fact that Stan Collymore did not make the impact Brian Little sought and then subsequently attracted the sort of headlines that his successor John Gregory correctly deplored, was a considerable disappointment to everyone and, as I observed earlier, illustrated graphically why team-building is as hazardous an occupation as it is expensive.

Collymore's arrival, followed by the signing of Simon Grayson from Leicester City, took Brian Little's spending to nigh on £30m with around £10m recouped by sales. Anyone who accused the club of 'not thinking big enough' would perhaps be taken aback by that equation at a time when huge outlay had also been necessary in refurbishing Villa Park.

All this wheeling and dealing had been carried out in a spirit of manager and chairman keeping each other informed and with the club's budget and wage structure firmly in mind. It had also resulted in the average age of the squad being substantially reduced and a well-balanced squad being carefully accumulated, bearing in mind the necessity to encourage our own quality young players, which the manager and coaching staff had done superbly well.

Under Little's management we had seen the likes of Michael Oakes, Riccardo Scimeca, Gareth Farrelly, Lee Hendrie, David Hughes, and others from our own youth scheme, given an opportunity to make progress in their careers. In the past, it seemed to me, we had not seen enough quality players of our own make their way.

Since the likes of Tony Daley and Steve Froggatt there had been something of a drought where the arrival of top-quality home-produced players was concerned (given that players such as Mark Bosnich, Ugo

Ehiogu and Dwight Yorke, were well into their teens when they joined us from other clubs).

The bottom line to all this, as season 1997-98 approached, was that my 'feel-good' factor about the future of the club and the way that all the various activities were being run, had never been more optimistic. One of the many things I have learned in seventy-four years of life and thirty-odd years in football is that few things are totally predictable. It is foolish to make predictions or promises because they can always rebound in your face.

Looking ahead we will simply continue to strive for new achievements. Looking back, this has not been an attempt to catalogue all of my experiences in chronological order, simply to recall what I trust are the most significant and interesting events as a substantial contribution to the club's modern history.

If I have added some life and personality to the facts and figures of the Aston Villa story, and in some areas given a new perspective, then the book is worthwhile.

I trust that my memory of previously unrecorded incidents and conversations has not become dimmed or in any way misshapen by the passing years. All descriptions are accurate as I recall them, in some cases, remember, decades after the event.

It was after I had started writing the book that the shocking news of Diana, the Princess of Wales's tragic car accident plunged not only the nation, but many parts of the world, into mourning. This inevitably brought back memories of the occasion when I was privileged to be introduced to her and prompted a reminder of meeting other world figures along the way.

Chapter Twenty

Falling For Royalty

Time, now, for a little name-dropping. Well, we all do it now and again don't we? Thirty years of access to well-known people does not remove the capacity to be star-struck once in a while, and why should it?

I don't mind admitting that I cherish the fact that being chairman of Aston Villa has led me into the company of some of the world's most famous people, including members of the Royal Family.

To name but three memorable examples I have been embarrassed while sitting next to Prince Charles, captivated by the late Diana, Princess of Wales, and awe-stricken by the South African President, Nelson Mandela. Involvement in charity work, for which we have our own Aston Villa Charitable Trust, and club tours, are possibly the major vehicles for meeting the non-football celebrities.

My proximity to Prince Charles arose from the period in the early 1990s when I was a committee member of the Prince's Trust.

Basically, each year we 'adopt' a particular charity to support substantially, in addition to all the smaller good causes which we help in many ways throughout any twelve months.

Thus, it was in my capacity as the Midlands' representative of the Prince's Trust, which covered a whole range of help for under-privileged teenagers with various needs, that I was invited with seven other similar representatives to have lunch with Prince Charles at Kensington Palace.

Readers will recall the time which was when his arm was in a sling as a result of a fall from his horse while playing polo. This 'arm-in-a-sling' appearance presented me with a simple point of contact to break the ice, not always easy on such occasions. I knew that he fished on a salmon beat not far from the one I frequented myself on the River Tay and I realised that his injury would be as big a handicap to him as an angler as it was as a polo player. "Have you had to stop salmon fishing, sir?" I asked him. "Not at all," he replied. "I'm learning to cast left-handed." To keep up the social chat I mentioned that, at around 8.30 one morning, whilst crossing a narrow bridge near the salmon beat, I had felt obliged to back off my Rolls to make way for a Range Rover crossing from the other direction. When the Range Rover passed me the driver, who was completely on his own, waved his thanks as he drove on and it was only then that I recognised the man at the wheel to be HRH himself.

Being the perfect host and diplomat that he undoubtedly is he claimed to remember the incident, though I must say I put this response down more to impeccable manners than expert memory. However, when it came time to sit down for our meal he asked me to sit next to him and I'm not ashamed to confess that I was thrilled by the invitation.

He was a very chatty neighbour during the meal and, at one point, he made some amusing comment which caused me to laugh and lean back onto the rear legs of my ornate, antique chair which, literally, came apart at the joints, depositing me onto the floor surrounded by precious Kensington Palace debris.

Embarrassed? What do YOU think? Yet the impeccable manners were quickly in evidence again as the demolished remains were removed and replaced with the minimum of fuss. The incident was quickly passed over and dismissed as a mere nothing.

Shortly afterwards, at another charitable event, this time a dinner for Turning Point charity, which is concerned with rehabilitating young offenders who have suffered from the effects of substance abuse, I was fortunate to be introduced to the Princess of Wales.

The function featured a concert by the violinist Nigel Kennedy, a dyed-in-the-wool Villa fanatic, at the Metropole Hotel. Master of Ceremonies was Dave Ismay, another staunch Villa supporter who was then a professional entertainer, but who was subsequently to undertake an important full-time staff role at Villa Park in charge of special projects.

In the light of her subsequent tragic death at the tender age of 36, the fact that I was to enjoy the delightful experience of meeting the Princess is more poignant in my memory than ever.

Deadly!

To my amazement and amusement when I was introduced to her she broke into that alluring laugh of hers which, at the time, could almost have been described as a girlish giggle, and said: "Oh, aren't you the one they call 'Deadly'?" I could only reply by saying "well, yes, I believe I am." But then, I added: "Did you hear about the antique chair I broke at Kensington Palace...?" This time she really did laugh, and replied: "Oh, it was YOU was it? Everyone was talking about it afterwards. It was a scream. I'm just glad it wasn't my chair. It was Maggie's." I'll never forget her saying: "It was Maggie's." It didn't strike me as being the ideal way for me to leave my mark on the Royal Household but, looking back on what proved to be her very high-profile and often sad life my everlasting memory will be of an enchanting, captivating young lady who truly was a light in everyone's lives. Diana, Princess of Wales, and that lovely smile.

Dave Ismay tells me that throughout the function she laughed, joked and chatted with those around her, visibly enjoying every moment of the occasion. The Princess was scheduled to go at a particular time but she declined to leave until after she had seen Jasper Carrott's cabaret.

Good for her... the People's Princess, she undoubtedly was.

Dave was subsequently in her company at another function and she told him that the Turning Point dinner was one of the happiest she had ever attended.

Meeting President Mandela, during the club's close season tour of South Africa in May 1994, left as indelible an impression on me for a rather different reason.

At a reception which he attended I was able to claim his attention to myself for maybe five minutes with his Ministers and minders some few yards away. My purpose was to discuss with him the importance of sporting contact between nations which can transcend any political activity in cementing friendships. In my opinion sport can make more progress in securing peace between nations than all the ambassadors and consulates that countries can provide.

No doubt, bearing in mind his lifetime spent fighting the obscenity of apartheid, he was more aware than anyone of how much the breakdown of South Africa's sporting involvement affected his country's relationship with the outside world. However, to confirm the point with more than mere words I offered to set in motion arrangements for a multi-racial football academy to be built in Johannesburg, to promote the coaching of excellence in football among young people.

As I pointed out, Aston Villa had already provided clinics to this end in Durban and Johannesburg. My manager, Ron Atkinson, and his coaches recognised the excellent skills of many South African youngsters who now needed professional coaching if they aspired to representing their country.

I asked Mr Mandela if he would agree to having such an academy entitled the Mandela Football Academy and he replied: "I would be honoured." During my meeting with him I was deeply impressed with his modesty and humility, given that he stands a very erect 6' 2" and kept his eyes firmly directed upon mine during the five minutes I spent alone in his company. I still find it difficult to believe that this man spent twenty-seven years in prison on Robin Island and came through the ordeal having retained his sanity and his sense of modesty alongside an undimmed imperial aura of the born leader.

Regrettably the academy scheme never came into being despite my ascertaining that, with the association of Nelson Mandela's name, bank finance would be available alongside major company conglomerates providing sponsorship to the tune of some £5m. When we returned to this country I informed the English FA, as a councillor, of the window of opportunity that had been opened up and though we sent two representatives out there on a fact-finding, logistical mission for ten days it was never followed through.

All I will add is that, in my confident view, if I had been able to afford the time to go to South Africa myself for the necessary period of time we could have made it happen. Maybe some of the kids from the townships would now be Premiership footballers and South African internationals.

Chapter Twenty-One

Brian Little: The Truth

On the afternoon of Tuesday February 24th, 1998 at around 2.30pm Brian Little walked into Steve Stride's office, dropped photo-copies of three newspaper articles on his desk and said: "I've had enough. I'm resigning. I would like you to inform the chairman for me because this time I do not want him to attempt to talk me round." The three cuttings were from morning newspapers which, presumably he had only just read, all of them critical of him and one of them in the Sun, written under the name of Andy Gray, his pal and former playing colleague. I got the impression that Andy's piece had particularly upset him.

My first knowledge of the sudden turn of events was when, after Brian had left his office, Steve telephoned me on his internal line to pass on the news, adding that he was sending Brian along to confirm that, indeed, he had made an irreversible decision to resign with immediate effect. I was told that Brian was absolutely adamant this time and there would be no talking him around. When Brian came to see me to confirm his decision I expressed my sadness and said I understood his reasoning.

Whatever else has been said or written about Brian's departure, those are the facts. No dispute, no mysterious happening behind the scenes, no abrasive comment from myself or anyone else at the club to prompt his leaving at a few minutes notice as he did. Brian Little left Aston Villa FC because he chose voluntarily to do so and because a variety of pressures about the job had brought him to the conclusion that it would be in the best interests of the club and himself if he moved on.

As for my own reaction, I was taken by surprise at the timing of his resignation, coming as it did only four days before a most critical period for us when we were to play Liverpool at home in the Premiership on the Saturday and Atlético Madrid in a UEFA Cup quarter-final first leg in Spain three days after that. Having said that, I could not claim to have been surprised at his actual decision to go, only the timing.

To explain what I mean by this and to further put the record straight it is necessary to give details of two very private meetings I had with him only ten days earlier, after our removal from the FA Cup by Coventry City which had further damaged a disappointing season during which we had gone out of the Coca Cola Cup at the first hurdle and slid disturbingly into relegation danger. It is my usual routine to go into the dressing room – win, lose or draw – to show my face ten to twenty minutes or so after a game in order to first allow a period of privacy between manager, coaches and players.

After the Coventry game the dressing room door was open but Brian Little was not inside. That was unusual. I found him in his room nearby with two or three of the coaching staff. When he saw me he asked them to leave, called me inside and locked the door behind us. "I've had enough," he told me, or similar words to those he subsequently used to Steve Stride. "I'm resigning." He added that, although he had not discussed it with his wife Heather, he felt it was in the best interests of Aston Villa that he should leave.

Here I do not wish to betray any confidences but it is fair to say in broad detail that he had been deeply affected by abuse suffered by his children who no longer wished to be taken to school because of it; by personal, foul-mouthed abuse he was receiving from members of the public seated near his dug-out place, where extra security men had been placed because of it; and by critical letters and articles in newspapers.

Poor results would also, no doubt, have played their part along with problems there had been with a number of players, some of whom had not been playing to their potential or the size of their transfer fees. It would be easy to speculate that Brian's confidence was taking something of a battering and my own observations led me to suspect that this was the case and was taking its toll.

Having spent all my working life in service industries, where people and staff are the stock in trade, I reckon I have become a semi-professional psychologist and as such I pay a great deal of attention to people's facial expressions. They can provide warning signs. Leading up to the time of his departure both myself and others noticed little things about Brian that suggested a declining confidence. This much was reflected in facial and physical reactions towards him from several senior players, particularly from the Christmas period onwards. The mood had changed in the dressing room and Brian was no doubt aware of it.

Despite by far the majority of the players literally 'loving' Brian Little as a man I believe that some of them had lost confidence in his ability to motivate them. He admitted as much when he resigned.

However, the bottom line of our chat after the Coventry defeat was my urging him not resign as a rash decision in the immediate disappointment of being knocked out of the cup but for him to reconsider, talk to Heather, and to come to my home the next morning for a heart-to-heart chat about things and to see how he felt then. The role of a chairman and board is to stand solidly behind their man, through good times and bad until such time as it becomes harmful to the prospects of the club to do so and we hadn't reached this stage with Brian. Indeed, we wanted him to enjoy more success.

My mind inevitably went back some twenty-eight years to the day Brian first joined the club as an apprentice. I well remember Brian's parents coming down from Tyneside and his mother telling me that he would not sign for us because he did not fancy being so far away from home. He was a very shy fifteen-year-old then, from a family of Newcastle supporters, and felt he would be happier staying in the north-east and signing for one of the local clubs up there who wanted him. I protested that this would be a bad mistake because Brian had obviously loved being with us for training and coaching. He had already been with our youth team abroad and there was no way he should sign for anyone else. Then Brian's mother observed that he might be persuaded to sign for Villa if his brother, Alan, could come too. She said that Alan was different to Brian who wanted to stay at home. I was assured by her that Alan would go anywhere and had the makings of a good professional so, just as in the case of the two Riochs, Bruce and Neil, we signed them both, despite the fact that when I checked with our chief scout at the time, he had no reports of Alan being of the necessary potential. In the event he made a couple of appearances for us, but went on to have a good career elsewhere and became a successful manager of York City.

As for Brian, we all know what an outstanding player he became and, because of the feeling that Villa were required to take good care of him as a fifteen-year-old, I had a kind of father-son relationship with him from then on and it was on a similar sort of basis that I chatted to him at my house on Sunday December 7th, 1997. The outcome was that he had calmed down and went home in a far more cheerful frame of mind than he had been the previous evening. He had decided to stay. So much for all those ill-informed 'did-he-leave-or-was-he-pushed' debates that went on when he resigned a second time.

OK, so now it was around three o'clock on the Tuesday afternoon, we were playing Liverpool at home on Saturday, we had lost our two previous Premiership games, at home to Manchester United and away to Wimbledon since the FA Cup exit, three defeats on the trot, we were only six points above the relegation zone with one more game played than the bottom three and we were one week away from the first leg of our UEFA Cup-tie in Madrid.

No, Brian's timing wasn't good. I felt he should have stayed, at least until the end of the season, but it was not to be and now we needed a replacement manager. And we needed one quickly. The first, and only concrete suggestion, came from Steve Stride. Earlier in the season we had suggested to Brian Little, when first-team coaching was being re-organised, that it would make sense to contact John Gregory, at Wycombe Wanderers where he was now manager, and sound him out about returning to his former job, because he had never been adequately replaced. When we appointed Brian, Allan Evans and John there was an attractive system of coaching in which ex-forward Brian took the forwards, ex-midfielder John took the midfielders, ex-defender Allan Evans took the defenders and ex-goalkeeper Paul Barron took the goalkeepers.

It all worked wonderfully until Gregory left.

Many people felt that his departure had been a factor in the team's decline in the Premiership but Brian had rejected the idea of his return on the grounds that he would take over the coaching himself from Kevin MacDonald, who had been moved from the second team coaching responsibilities after John Gregory's departure.

Later Brian promoted Tony McAndrew from the youth team post and, while there were impressive performances in the UEFA Cup, inconsistencies in the Premiership continued to undermine all else and it was difficult to refute the feeling in many quarters that Gregory had never been adequately replaced. Kevin MacDonald and Tony McAndrew are both excellent coaches who remained on our staff, but the proof of the pudding at first team level in particular, is in results, and ours hadn't been good. Even so we remained fully committed behind Brian Little until he chose to leave.

Against this background, and with time against us, Steve Stride batted hard for Gregory's return. Meanwhile, we contacted the financial director Mark Ansell on his mobile almost the moment his feet touched the ground at Heathrow when he arrived back from a long weekend abroad. Anyone who carried on believing that Brian Little's departure and John Gregory's arrival had been set up beforehand would have thought very differently had they seen the emergency exercise that went on behind the scenes.

Quickly an informal board meeting was summoned as Mark Ansell sped up the M1 and, in these discussions I made the point that, while I was also an admirer of John Gregory's coaching calibre, if we were to appoint him we would be castigated in the media and by a section of supporters for not appointing a 'big name'. It was not a case of disagreeing with the feeling that his return would be beneficial, simply of playing the Devil's Advocate in expressing the opposite point of view for discussion.

By this time the news of Brian's departure had appeared on Ceefax and Teletext and on local radio and would shortly be hitting the major news bulletins. Already I was getting telephone calls from second and third-party intermediaries telling me that such-and-such a 'Big-Name' manager would like to come to Villa but who couldn't apply in person because he was already in a job, or whatever. They were expecting me to go to them. The so-called 'deadly' reputation of mine doesn't seem to put these 'Big Names' off when there is an attractive vacancy on offer.

Just to give an example of the kind of speculation that goes on in these situations, the *Evening Mail* next day ran a phone-in service to enable their readers to phone for the 'candidate' of their choice. There were twelve 'possibles' on their list, namely: Terry Venables, Bobby Robson, Andy Gray, Graham Taylor, Gerry Francis, Allan Evans, Bruce Rioch, Ruud Gullit, David Platt, Martin O'Neill, John Toshack and Radomir Antic. Before their phone-in lines even began to hum we were at the nearby New Hall Hotel with John Gregory discussing the terms of his contract and, by telephone, the compensation we would pay to Wycombe Wanderers for the remainder of his contract.

The previous evening we had unanimously agreed that an approach to

John would be made provided we received permission from the Wycombe Wanderers chairman, Ivor Beeks, and his board. We asked Steve Stride to 'get on his bike' down the M5 to meet up with John in a hotel in Bristol where Wycombe Wanderers were preparing for a Second Division fixture with Bristol Rovers. I would have gone with him, but the first important action was to make the chairman-to-chairman contact. Steve had his mobile telephone switched on to comply with our mutual agreement that, if Mr Beeks declined our approach, then he would turn around and come back and we would turn our attention elsewhere. In the event Mr Beeks, a builder in High Wycombe, said that he was very sad to be losing such an outstanding young manager, and engaging personality, but he would not stand in John's way of taking such an opportunity at a major club. This was the green light for Steve to continue down the motorway, meet up with John at the hotel in Bristol and arrange for him to meet us at 10am the next morning. Steve, Mark and myself met at New Hall an hour before his arrival, to talk all the details through.

Contract talks with John presented little difficulty, such was his enthusiasm to return to Aston Villa, a club he had loved with all the commitment of a supporter since his playing days, when he was signed from Northampton Town by Ron Saunders. Agreeing compensation with Wycombe by telephone took a little longer, but after a couple of hours of 'phone calls back and forth all was amicably settled and John Gregory replaced Brian Little, approximately twenty-four hours after the latter's shock departure, on a three-year contract.

By four o'clock we were unveiling our new manager before a surprised media corps, leaving him just two full days to prepare to meet Liverpool.

Even then the whirlwind nature of it all was not over. That same evening our reserves were playing Preston North End, whose reserve team coach was none other than Steve Harrison, another former Villa coach as my earlier reminiscences have described, and the very man John wanted as his right-hand man. The reserve game also afforded the opportunity for some adverse public reaction to manifest itself in the form of a rowdy group congregating in the car park under my office window to hurl loud-mouthed obscenities in my direction for a considerable period of time. Efforts by our security chief, John Hood, to get them to disperse proved ineffective. I eventually went down to confront them and slowly the demo broke up. Interestingly, I'm told that these 'fans' did not follow my own lead in then taking a seat in the stadium to watch our reserves in action.

DEADLY!

Predictably the accusation of 'not appointing a Big Name' cropped up in the newspapers next day and I was assailed by carefully-selected anti-Ellis 'fans' on Central's Thursday night *Late Tackle* programme. It was interesting to note how people were prepared to jump to entirely the wrong conclusions about the manner of Brian Little's departure and to deal in innuendo suggesting that Brian had been 'pushed'. Even when Brian himself gave interviews to local and national newspapers describing in detail how this was not the case, those who chose to disbelieve us both, preferring to dwell on the 'Deadly strikes again' theory, did so despite all of the factual statements to the contrary. Once again I was reminded of my repeated experience that when things go right the manager is a hero, when they go wrong the chairman is a villain.

Football is very much a case of the mood of the moment and that mood can change even more quickly than in politics. Within little more than a month of John Gregory's arrival we had taken twelve points out of fifteen, with the same set of players who had previously lost three matches on the trot, remember, and those dissenting supporters and the media folk who had shared their foreboding, were starting to wonder whether we now had a 'Big Name' in the making. Speaking personally I could only hope so. John Gregory's two predecessors had won us a trophy, made good progress in the Premiership, for their first couple of seasons and had then slipped back. What I have always sought for Aston Villa is a lengthy period of prolonged success, something that has never been achieved in modern times.

Looking ahead to season 1998-99, what are the chances of John Gregory beginning to bring us the consistency on the field that I personally felt would be achieved by Brian Little? No-one would expect me to make such a prediction, nor would I be foolish enough to commit one of a chairman's worst crimes, that of passing the dreaded vote of confidence. What I will say is that we were all impressed with his positive manner, with the instant lift in mood he achieved in the dressing room, with the kind of goal-scoring football his team played right from day one, and with the kind of comments he made to the media.

One example of his 'let's go for it' attitude was when we raised the possibility of gaining late entry to the InterToto Cup, simply because its change of date to late July from June and its incentive of a UEFA Cup place for the winner, made it a far more attractive proposition than it had been before.

This had been brought home to us when we played Bordeaux in the first round of the UEFA Cup in 1997-98 and realised that this was how their place in the competition had been secured. John was instantly prepared to give it a go for all the positive reasons. After the final match of the season, an excellent 1-0 victory over Arsenal, sandwiched between the Gunners becoming FA Premiership champions and attempting to complete the double, John Gregory's record in the league amounted to twenty-seven points from a possible thirty-three, a splendid start by any yardstick.

Misleadingly at that time, as it was to emerge, the final whistle of our season ended in an air of frustration as the news came through that Chris Sutton, who scored a first-half hat-trick against us in our first home match of the season, had scored an 88th minute goal for Blackburn against Newcastle at Ewood Park to hold on to what could well have been the final UEFA Cup place.

Off we went to give the players a well-earned holiday, now clinging to the hope that Chelsea would beat Stuttgart in the final of the Cup Winners' Cup and thus relinquish the UEFA Cup place (already earned by their winning the Coca Cola Cup), thereby pushing the qualifying places in the Premiership down to seventh... and Aston Villa!

The lovely Mediterranean sunshine island of Majorca holds some very special memories for me, as I have outlined earlier in these pages, but few rate as more pleasurable than the balmy night of Wednesday, May 13th, 1998. As the Cup Winners' Cup final was played out John Gregory and his staff preferred to sit outside the hotel relaxing rather than put up with the tension of watching the final screened from Stockholm. Not me. I was in there glued to the TV set for every kick and yes, we did enjoy an extra little holiday celebration after Gianfranco Zola had left his subs' seat to score his magnificent winning goal. To be honest I found myself leaping what felt like six feet from my seat to punch the air before rushing outside to tell the others the news. Then the realisation dawned that there was still some time to go so back I went to sweat through the finishing stages.

When the final whistle sounded I nipped outside again to tell John Gregory and now it was his turn to leap several feet into the air before flinging his arms around me for a victory dance followed by the popping of a few champagne corks. What an achievement it was to earn that qualifying place.

To most of the rest of Europe that goal simply meant that Chelsea were winners of the Cup Winners' Cup. Full stop. For Aston Villa it meant that. And much, much more. We were back in Europe by the 'front door', with no need to play in the InterToto competition while, as a club, we had been restored among the elite of European competitors by the excellent transformation under John Gregory. We had climbed eight Premiership places from 15th and the threat of relegation on February 28th, to seventh and a place in Europe all in the space of eleven matches. I've no idea how many clubs have changed from relegation fodder into European contenders in little more than a couple of months, but that was the sensation we were able to savour as a new Majorcan memory was taken on board.

So far, so good. If he proves to be my last manager, and we enjoy a lengthy chairman-manager relationship, punctuated by success on the field, no-one will be a happier man than Herbert Douglas Ellis.

Chapter Twenty-Two

So Much Still To Do

Nigh on thirty years have ticked away since my first, fact-finding knock on Aston Villa's door and with each tick of the clock the stadium and the atmosphere within, as yet more significant improvements lie ahead, have been an integral part of an explosion of new interest in the game.

Premiership football, and indeed the game at a lower level, is now a multi-billion pound business which simply seems to grow and grow in public demand and interest each season. In tandem with these booming years the general public has an absolute right to expect everything we do to be of the very highest specification.

Nowadays, and for many years past, visitors are greeted to the North Stand main office entrance, with the utmost courtesy, by our telephonist-receptionists Marie and Margaret or any other member of staff with whom they come into contact, unlike the bad old, pre-1968 days.

Marie Priest has been the public's first contact with the club for 17 years. Margaret Ward joined her ten years ago.

The pair simply amaze telephone callers by recognising the multitude of regulars, among the thousands of telephone calls they answer each week, without any self-introduction being necessary, those who call in person, for whatever reason, are equally treated as the important people they are.

As outlined earlier in the book my philosophy as a travel agent, a professional in the service industry, remember, similar to football, was that when you are dealing with a paying public you have to do whatever is necessary, within reason, to keep those customers happy. Consequently all of the staff are expected to operate in this way and it is how callers are treated, by members of staff who know their business inside out and care about Aston Villa's good name and reputation. This is especially true on match-days, when our part-time stewards, car park attendants and security staff have earned a reputation from visitors of all descriptions for their courtesy and efficiency.

If it is the club secretary who is required then Steve Stride, now also a director, has been on Villa's staff for a quarter-of-a-century. Steve is assisted by his own secretary, Pam Silk, who has been with the club approximately as long as he has; while the former assistant secretary, Arthur Moseley, another long-serving employee, retired only recently after 20 years of service.

In an adjacent office, Debbie Ritchie, the manager's secretary has put in 21 years of service; while, in accounts, my trusty financial facts-and-figures man, Phil Longmore, has been with us fourteen years.

Mark McGuiness, also in accounts, is another 20-year employee. At the helm in the ticket office is former West Bromwich Albion defender Ray Fairfax who, along with Lee Preece and an excellent staff, distributes tickets for both big games and the routine ones, with rare good humour. Lee was more recently promoted to the role vacated by Arthur Moseley when he retired after the second leg against Atlético Madrid.

Another 21-year employee is Abdul Rashid, the commercial manager. Abdul introduced himself to Villa Park, according to his own version of events, as a bit of a nuisance hanging around the old souvenir shop, collecting badges, as a local schoolboy and pestering staff to find him odd jobs to do. Abdul left school, joined the staff, made his way rung-by-rung to the head of his department and has helped us to raise many millions of pounds with many more to come, I'm sure. If he truly was a 'nuisance' in the 1970s I can only say he is a rare asset twenty years on.

Also on the fund-raising side, with a long good-service record is John Greenfield, now head of merchandising at the Villa Village and formerly a lottery rep. John has also helped move thousands of fans around this country and abroad by means of the travel club and, like the others, has claret-and-blue blood in his veins.

Our safety/operations manager John Hood, an ex-police chief superintendent, has joined us more recently, but he has helped to make Villa Park's security a role model in this country and abroad.

So Much Still To Do

One department head who seems to have been with me forever is Stadium Manager, Ted Small who, as I described early in these memoirs, was one of the local tradesmen to step in and help the club when we needed it most in 1968-69. Ted has done twenty-five years with me and literally saved the club millions of pounds. As one example the Doug Ellis stand was virtually rebuilt as an in-house project with Ted supervising a team of tradesmen in the construction rather than employing an outside building company at huge expense. By comparison with five quotations we had received from national construction companies we saved for the club a sum of £1.8m. Then there is the groundsman, Tony Eden, a former Villa and Walsall player, who has battled against the elements for seventeen years to look after our playing surface. These days Tony's so-called Garden of Eden can be warmed by a state-of-the-art under-soil heating system and has been newly-sown with a mixture of real grass binding its roots around tough artificial fibres. Nicely bedded down and with its own 'hot water bottle' the grass has never looked greener for Aston Villa FC.

Many part-time employees have also served the club nobly for lengthy periods, notably our tour guide Jackie Watts, who has shown thousands of visitors from across this country and, indeed, the world, around Villa Park before sending them off entertained and far better informed from his 65 years of support and encyclopaedic memory of the club history.

Alongside all these people are many other loyal employees and claret-and-blue servants who are no less valued for not having been mentioned here by name. Perhaps the most notable of all was dear, old Eric Houghton, Mr Aston Villa himself, who before his death on May 1st, 1996, had served the club as an England international forward and in almost every other appropriate capacity up to director level, for an amazing seventy years.

Our new Former Players' Association, under the leadership of Neil Rioch, is instrumental in dozens of ex-players retaining their links with the club. Aston Villa FC does seem to inspire a lifelong affinity in this way.

Then, as if I could ever forget, there is Marion Stringer. Marion has been my secretary and personal assistant for some 20 years dating back to when she first began to work for me at Ellmanton Construction.

I know it may sound a touch corny, something of a cliché, to say that someone is 'indispensable', but I truly could not manage without her.

Marion knows everything about my way of working, always

recognising the truth of the plaque on my desk that warns: "Beware, subject to mood changes without notice." She knows when to keep her head down and say nothing, when to offer advice, when to keep callers at bay, how to be discreet with the media.

And, yes, I have told her that I could not manage without her and her reply is typically self-effacing, like: "The graveyards are full of 'indispensable' staff, Mr Ellis." Of all her many qualities, maybe her sense of humour is her strongest point. My secretary, Sharon Barnhurst, has been with us for ten years and she works alongside Marion to form a duet who keep my diary and my secretarial work ticking over efficiently, whatever the demands in time and effort. However, I simply cannot mention everyone who deserves it here but if I am truly proud of any one feature of my many years at Villa Park it is that so many top-class employees have chosen to stay on board and help to make the club all that it has become. Steve Stride has described us as 'one big happy family'. Old Deadly can't be too bad to work for! So here I am, at 74, still striving to make Aston Villa one of the most successful clubs in the country on and off the field. So much to do, so little time, as they say. By the end of season 1997-98 our new Holte End entertaining suite of facilities, with its state-of-the-art kitchen and capacity to seat and serve 650 with silver service, was taking off in the care of an excellent marketing and catering staff . It is the second largest such facility in Birmingham and a main plank in our capacity to serve 2,700 meals on a match day. Equally our ground catering is also first-class and in very good hands. Also, we are currently awaiting planning permission to transform Bodymoor Heath from being merely one of the best training grounds in the country into a true, residential Football Academy with all the necessary additional facilities and also to carry out further, major improvements at Villa Park.

I have been asked who will take over the reins when the day arrives for me to retire. The answer is that, when the time comes my successor will have emerged through the ranks of the board, probably as it is already constituted. Since we strengthened numerically and in terms of expertise for the purposes of flotation we have excellent directors, including the company secretary, Steve Stride.

The latest acquisitions: David Owen the legal expert, Mark Ansell the financial specialist and Tony Hales, the chief executive of Allied Domecq plc, add to a selection of high-calibre commercial and professional men, each well-qualified to be regarded, especially as their experience grows, as a possible future chairman. Our President is former director Tony Alderson, a retired senior partner of Edge & Ellison, the club lawyers, while Senior Vice President is Mervyn King, the Deputy Governor of the Bank of England – all devoted long-term supporters of Aston Villa FC.

What is more they are all pulling in the same direction for the long-term good of the club, not pulling apart with petty jealousies like in the 'bad old days'. Which is roughly where I came in...

So, when WILL I retire? All I can say is that I will know when such a time has arrived, if and when I can no longer make the necessary executive decisions on finance and other important matters. Just now any such thoughts are far, far from my mind.

If I can be excused for indulging myself in the unfulfilled fantasy of my youth, when I longed but failed to be a star footballer, perhaps my best, tongue-in-cheek answer is that I would be content to believe that, one day, I will die with my football boots on, and Aston Villa will be a major force in world football.

THE 30-YEAR PROFIT AND LOSS

Aston Villa's relevant financial facts and figures since the Boardroom changes of 1968/69 are:

YEAR	NET PROFIT/(LOSS) AFTER TAX	TOTAL TURNOVER	FOOTBALL INCOME	COMMERCIAL & OTHERS	TRANSFER FEE SURPLUS (DEFICIT)	TOTAL WAGES COST
1997/98	£7,915,000	£31,769,000	£12,171,000	£19,598,000	£942,000	£(12,388,000)
1996/97	£(2,717,000)	£22,079,000	£9,038,000	£13,041,000	£(9,336,000)	£(10,070,000)
1995/96	£(63,000)	£18,865,000	£8,757,000	£10,108,000	£(5,851,000)	£(7,717,000)
1994/95	£2,270,000	£13,001,000	£6,473,000	£6,528,000	£668,000	£(7,139,000)
1993/94	£509,000	£13,014,000	£6,863,000	£6,151,000	£(2,311,000)	£(6,248,000)
1992/93	£(209,000)	£10,175,000	£5,503,000	£4,672,000	£(3,197,000)	£(4,498,000)
1991/92	£2,425,000	£7,453,000	£3,913,000	£3,550,000	£2,876,000	£(4,411,000)
1990/91	£985,000	£7,208,000	£3,621,000	£3,587,000	£(910,000)	£(2,457,000)
1989/90	£624,682	£5,555,199	£3,111,276	£2,443,923	£(629,105)	£(2,608,874)
1988/89	£799,704	£4,015,888	£2,121,877	£1,894,011	£(22,695)	£(1,609,305)
1987/88	£(92,646)	£2,683,087	£1,570,781	£1,112,306	£(54,930)	£(1,714,507)
1986/87	£(176,335)	£2,081,376	£1,325,386	£755,990	£(177,810)	£(1,183,024)
1985/86	£(199,575)	£2,121,352	£1,264,345	£857,007	£(477,750)	£(1,057,058)
1984/85	£254,176	£1,912,377	£1,122,438	£789,939	£242,000	£(1,181,556)
1983/84	£293,917	£2,233,805	£1,429,418	£804,387	£48,491	£(1,124,558)
1982/83	£(475,045)	£2,267,469	£1,435,561	£831,908	£(450,250)	£(1,202,912)
1981/82	£243,242	£2,630,138	£1,711,346	£918,792	£(42,500)	£(1,104,360)
1980/81	£246,915	£2,083,965	£1,315,618	£768,347	£450,000	£(1,131,378)
1979/80	£372,096	£1,704,553	£1,141,170	£563,383	£1,051,500	£(953,679)
1978/79	£(182,862)	£1,519,559	£1,059,377	£460,182	£(32,000)	£(671,421)
1977/78	£(420,081)	£1,477,136	£1,212,982	£264,154	£(433,576)	£(466,005)
1976/77	£279,856	£1,272,934	£1,114,571	£158,363	£(27,748)	£(463,737)
1975/76	£(135,014)	£847,154	£715,023	£132,131	£(298,912)	£(295,396)
1974/75	£(94,867)	£544,936	£458,152	£86,784	£(129,151)	£(280,379)
1973/74	£123,172	£362,134	£295,996	£66,138	£129,966	£(189,740)
1972/73	£(31,963)	£383,141	£324,653	£58,488	£(63,858)	£(169,699)
1971/72	£(91,085)	£383,808	£335,843	£47,965	£(167,153)	£(180,289)
1970/71	£77,506	£344,848	£306,959	£37,889	£(6,770)	£(140,000)
1969/70	£(175,136)	£262,335	£221,380	£40,955	£211,267	£(126,149)
1968/69	£(67,508)	£198,256	£180,759	£17,497	£75,296	£(95,554)
1967/68	£(46,070)	£150,720	£139,454	£11,266	£(68,173)	£(89,252)

★ *Sums in brackets denote a deficit.*

Where Are They Now?

(a random look at the whereabouts of some of the main personalities mentioned in these pages)

AUDREY, my first wife... still a good friend, residing in Four Oaks.

WILLIE ANDERSON... living in the United States, working on TV promotion.

CHARLIE AITKEN... Villa Park regular, residing in West Midlands.

RON ATKINSON... TV analyst, residing in Barnt Green.

TONY BARTON... deceased.

RON BENDALLL... deceased.

ALAN BENNETT... semi-retired in Leicestershire while retaining Leicester City connection.

BRIAN CLOUGH... retired and residing in East Midlands.

HARRY CRESSMAN... Retired and residing in the Bahamas.

VIC CROWE... Villa regular, retired and residing in Sutton Coldfield.

STAN CULLIS... retired and residing in West Midlands.

JIM CUMBES... commercial manager at Lancashire County Cricket Club.

TOMMY DOCHERTY... popular after-dinner speaker.

DOREEN... my sister... residing in Chedworth, Gloucestershire.

SIR WILLIAM DUGDALE... landowner in Coleshill-Atherstone area.

BRIAN EVANS... still a Villa fanatic. Property conveyance specialist, residing in Sutton Coldfield.

SIR TOM FINNEY... President of Preston North End.

BRIAN GODFREY... still a Villa man at heart, living and working in Gloucestershire.

JIMMY GREAVES... media freelance residing in Essex.

PHIL 'TIGER' HART... deceased.

JIM HARTLEY... deceased.

HARRY KARTZ... retired and residing in West Midlands and Florida.

BRIAN LITTLE... manager of Stoke City.

PAT MATTHEWS... a businessman residing in Marbella.

ROY McLAREN... residing in Australia.

BILLY McNEIL... residing in Scotland.

JOE MERCER... deceased.

BRUCE NORMANSELL... still a Villa man, residing in West Midlands.

HARRY PARKES... runs his sports outfitters business in Birmingham.

BRUCE RIOCH... manager of Norwich City.

NEIL RIOCH... instigator of Aston Villa Former Players Association, residing in West Midlands and running his own business.

RON SAUNDERS... retired and still residing in Knowle.

GRAEME SOUNESS... Benfica coach, in Lisbon.

TONY STEPHENS... based in Meriden, representing top players including Alan Shearer, Dwight Yorke and Michael Owen.

DICK TAYLOR... deceased.

GRAHAM TAYLOR... back at Watford FC and teamed up again in renewed successful partnership with Elton John.

PETER TAYLOR... deceased.

BRIAN TILER... killed in road accident, Italy 1990.

GRAHAM TURNER... manager of Hereford United.

Dr. JOZEF VENGLOS... actively involved in football in Slovakia.

JACK WISEMAN... vice-chairman of Birmingham City FC after a spell as chairman.

RON WYLIE... head of Aston Villa's community affairs.